EYEWITNESS
FOSSIL

D0539469

C334099309

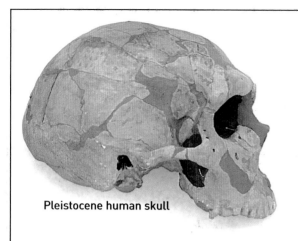
Pleistocene human skull

Eocene gastropods

Eocene fish

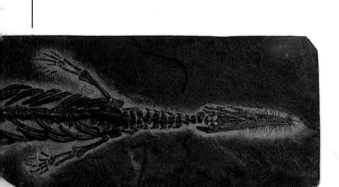
Triassic swimming reptile

Cretaceous dinosaur
finger bones

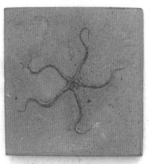
Jurassic brittlestar

Cretaceous
cone (sectioned
and polished)

Cretaceous cone

Ordovician nautiloid
(polished and shaped)

Jurassic sea urchin

Modern
horsetail

Carboniferous
horsetail

Eocene
shark
tooth

Pleistocene coral

Carboniferous fern

Jurassic
ammonite (carved
as a snakestone)

EYEWITNESS
FOSSIL

Written by
DR PAUL D TAYLOR

Triassic dinosaur
footprint

Carboniferous
lycopod

Eocene fish

Silurian
brachiopod

Pleistocene
handaxe

Permian tree fern
(sectioned and polished)

Pliocene scallop

Modern coral

In association with
THE NATURAL HISTORY
MUSEUM, LONDON

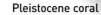

Pleistocene coral

Cretaceous
dinosaur tooth

Jurassic
ammonite

Carboniferous
spider

Pleistocene
sea urchin

Cretaceous
opalized
bivalve

Cretaceous opalized
gastropod

Cretaceous
worm tube

Cretaceous bryozoan

Jurassic coral (sectioned
and polished)

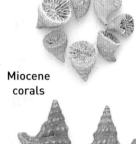
Miocene
corals

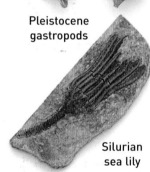
Pleistocene
gastropods

19th-century
microscope
for examining
thin sections

Silurian
sea lily

DK | Penguin Random House

Project editor Louise Pritchard   Art editor Alison Anholt-White
Senior editor Sophie Mitchell   Senior art editor Julia Harris
Editorial director Sue Unstead   Art director Anne-Marie Bulat
Special photography Colin Keates (Natural History Museum, London)

PAPERBACK EDITION
Managing editors Linda Esposito, Andrew Macintyre
Managing art editor Jane Thomas   Category publisher Linda Martin
Art director Simon Webb   Editor and reference compiler Clare Hibbert
Art editor Joanna Pocock   Consultant Kim Bryan   Production Jenny Jacoby
Picture research Celia Dearing   DTP designer Siu Yin Ho

RELAUNCH EDITION

DK DELHI
Project Editor Priyanka Kharbanda   Project Art Editor Neha Sharma
Assistant Editor Antara Raghavan   Assistant Art Editor Priyanka Bansal
DTP Designer Pawan Kumar   Senior DTP Designer Harish Aggarwal
Picture Researcher Sakshi Saluja   Jacket Designer Juhi Sheth
Managing Editor Kingshuk Ghoshal   Managing Art Editor Govind Mittal

DK LONDON
Senior Art Editor Spencer Holbrook   Editor Anna Streiffert Limerick
Jacket Editor Claire Gell   Jacket Design Development Manager Sophia MTT
Producer, pre-production David Almond   Producer Gary Batchelor
Managing Editor Francesca Baines   Managing Art Editor Philip Letsu
Publisher Andrew Macintyre   Associate Publishing Director Liz Wheeler
Art Director Karen Self   Design Director Philip Ormerod
Publishing Director Jonathan Metcalf

This Eyewitness ® Guide has been conceived by
Dorling Kindersley Limited and Editions Gallimard

This edition published in 2017
Hardback edition first published in Great Britain in 1990.
Paperback edition first published in Great Britain in 2003 by
Dorling Kindersley Limited
80 Strand, London, WC2R 0RL

Copyright © 1990, 2003, 2017 Dorling Kindersley Limited
A Penguin Random House Company
10 9 8 7 6 5 4 3 2 1
001 – 299423 – June/2017

All rights reserved.
No part of this publication may be reproduced, stored in or introduced into a retrieval system,
or transmitted, in any form, or by any means (electronic, mechanical, photocopying, recording,
or otherwise), without the prior written permission of the copyright owner.

A CIP catalogue record for this book is available from the British Library.
ISBN 978-0-2412-8687-6

Printed and bound in China

A WORLD OF IDEAS:
SEE ALL THERE IS TO KNOW

www.dk.com

Slide of thin section of
Carboniferous bryozoans

Modern
magnolia flower

Miocene bat jaws

Contents

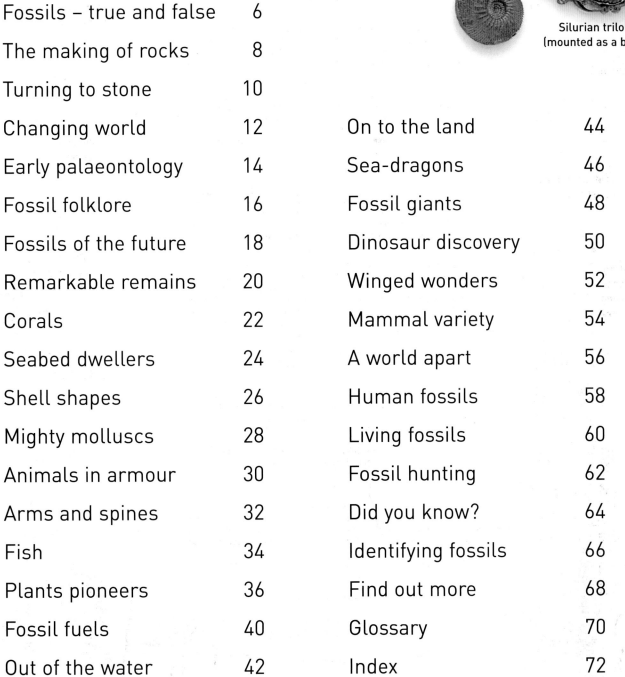

Jurassic ammonites

Silurian trilobite (mounted as a brooch)

Fossils – true and false

Fossil collections
People have collected fossils for centuries. This illustration appeared in an Italian book published in 1670.

Fossils are the remains or evidence of animals or plants that have been preserved naturally. They range from the skeletons of huge dinosaurs to tiny plants and animals. Most fossils are formed from the hard parts of animals and plants, such as shells, bones, teeth, or wood. Footprints, eggs, and burrows can be fossilized, too. The study of fossils, called palaeontology, shows us that life began on Earth 3.5 billion years ago. Fossils of extinct species give us a rare glimpse of ancient life.

Only bones
The only remains of animals are often hard bones. This fossilized vertebra is from a plesiosaur, an ancient swimming reptile.

Trilobite cast and mould

Taking shape
Fossils can have two parts. A rotting animal leaves a hollow mould, which can fill up with sediment to form a hard cast.

Rare delicacy
Detailed fossils of dead plants are rare because plants rot quickly. However, the veins in this leaf have been preserved.

Pearly ammonite
Ammonites are now extinct. They were animals that had hard shells made of a chalky mineral called aragonite.

Plesiosaur tooth

Tough tooth
Teeth are often fossilized as they are hard.

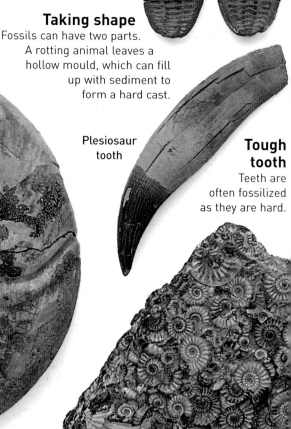

Precious wood
One type of fossilization occurs when chemical changes make a mineral grow instead of the original animal or plant tissues, or material. The tissues of this fossilized wood have been replaced by opal.

Ancient trail

This image shows the trail of an animal moving across the seabed millions of years ago. Fossilized evidence of animal activities are called trace fossils.

False fossil

This is not a fossil. The tree-like growths, called dehdrites, are manganese in the rock.

Packed tight

Some fossils are densely packed because the animals lived in large numbers. These ammonites are in limestone.

Unnatural burial

This Ancient Greek pot was found in the ground, but it is not a fossil. Fossil, which means "something dug up", once described buried pottery and minerals, but they are no longer considered fossils.

Area where fragments are missing

Easy mistake

These images do not show a fossilized duck head and a human leg! Their shape is pure chance. They are really lumps of rock called flint nodules found in chalk. The shapes of flint nodules can be very peculiar and are often mistaken for fossils.

Flint "duck's head"

Flint "human leg"

Animal or vegetable?

No – mineral! Minerals are not the remains of an animal or plant, and are therefore not fossils.

Fossil fakes

During the 1720s, when the nature of fossils was unclear, these "fossils" were carved and buried in the ground by people trying to fool a scientist named Johann Beringer. He was taken in and published descriptions of his find, but was later humiliated when the hoax was revealed.

"Bunch of grapes"

"Squid-like creature"

Beringer's "Lying Stones"

The making of rocks

The rocks beneath us have been forming for 4 billion years. Earth's crust is made up of elements, particularly oxygen, silicon, iron, aluminium, calcium, sodium, carbon, magnesium, and potassium. These combine to form minerals. Rocks are made of minerals. They can be metamorphic, sedimentary, or igneous.

Amethyst
This is the purple mineral quartz, with hexagonal (six-sided) crystals.

Folded rock
Movements in Earth's crust can make rocks crack, forming faults, or buckle, forming folds.

Feldspar
Mica
Quartz

Black mica
Glassy quartz
White feldspar

Granite
Granite is an igneous rock formed at great depths.

Distorted trilobite

Twisted trilobite
Metamorphic rocks may contain distorted fossils, such as this trilobite in slate.

Thin section of granite

Band rich in mica
Band rich in quartz

Molten rocks

Igneous rocks are formed by cooled molten magma deep inside Earth. Magma may erupt from volcanoes before it cools, but cooling often occurs underground.

Hot rocks

Heat and pressure create metamorphic rocks. Marble is metamorphosed limestone, while slate is metamorphosed shale.

Layer upon layer
The USA's Grand Canyon, formed by eroded sandstone and limestone, is a natural slice through Earth's crust. The oldest layer is at the bottom.

Schist
Parallel bands of minerals feature on metamorphic rocks. Schist forms from shale or mud.

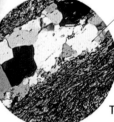

Band of quartz
Band of silicate minerals

Thin section of schist

One varve
Fine sediment
Coarse sediment

Rock bands
In this sedimentary rock, each set of one light layer (fine sediment) and one dark layer (coarse sediment) is a year's accumulation of silt and mud, called a varve, at the bottom of a glacier-fed lake.

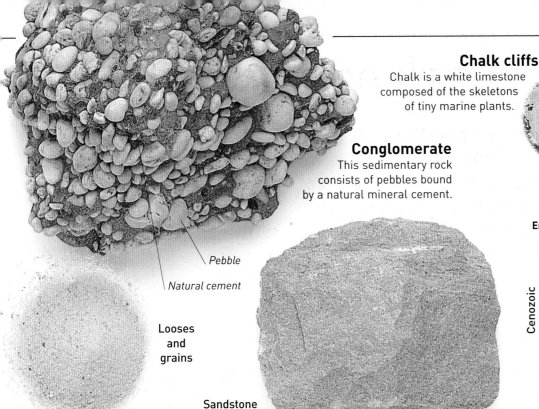

Conglomerate
This sedimentary rock consists of pebbles bound by a natural mineral cement.

Pebble

Natural cement

Looses and grains

Sandstone

Deposited rocks
Rocks are continually being eroded, creating grains carried by river, sea, or wind. They are deposited, together with the remains of animals and plants, as mud, sand, or coarser material. When this sediment is buried deeper, it becomes compacted and cemented to form sedimentary rock.

Quartz

Iron-rich cement

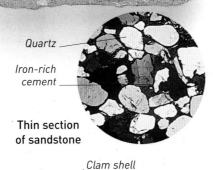

Thin section of sandstone

Clam shell

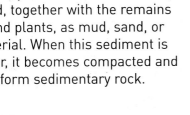

From rock to rock
As cliffs of sedimentary rocks are eroded, small pieces are deposited on the beach to later form new sedimentary rock.

Fossil container
Many sedimentary rocks contain lumps called concretions or nodules. These formed around fossil shells like this clam.

Shell fragment

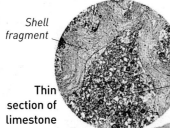

Thin section of limestone

Finely broken shells

Fossiliferous rock
Limestone is a sedimentary rock composed of calcite and other carbonate minerals. The calcite is derived from the shells and skeletons of marine animals and plants. This Silurian limestone contains fossil brachiopods (see pp.24–25).

Fossil brachiopod

Era	Period	Million years ago
Cenozoic	Holocene (Epoch)	0.01
	Pleistocene (Epoch)	2
	Pliocene (Epoch)	5
	Miocene (Epoch)	24
	Oligocene (Epoch)	34
	Eocene (Epoch)	55
	Palaeocene (Epoch)	65
Mesozoic	Cretaceous	142
	Jurassic	206
	Triassic	248
Palaeozoic	Permian	290
	Carboniferous	354
	Devonian	417
	Silurian	443
	Ordovician	495
	Cambrian	545
	Precambrian (about seven times longer than all the other periods put together)	4,600 (origin of Earth)

Stratigraphical column
A series of eras and periods describe the age of rocks and fossils.

Turning to stone

The process of changing from a living organism to a fossil takes millions of years. As soon as animals and plants die, they begin to rot. Hard parts, such as the shells, bones, and teeth of animals, or the wood of plants, last longer than soft tissue, but they are often scattered by animals, wind, or water. For fossilization to take place, an animal or plant must be buried quickly by sediment. Only a tiny fraction will ever be found.

Land shapes
Over millions of years rocks are eroded, bringing ancient fossils to the surface.

2 Decaying mussel
When a mussel dies, two chalky shells open out into a "butterfly" position. The soft parts of the mussel inside the shells begin to rot, or are eaten by animals.

Living mussel

Byssal threads

1 Living mussel
Mussels live in the sea, attached to rocks by byssal threads. Dense masses form mussel beds. If a mussel becomes detached it may die.

From preservation to discovery

These four drawings show how animals can be preserved and their remains discovered millions of years later. It is a slow process, and the climate and shape of the land will change as much as the animal and plant life.

1. Dead animals sink to the seabed and the remains are buried by layers of sediment

2. Lower layers of sediment turn to rock, and the remains harden to form fossils

3. The rock is folded and eroded

4. The fossils are exposed on the surface

Soft parts have rotted away

3 Hard parts remain
When the soft parts of the mussel have rotted away, the hard parts – that is – the shells, remain.

4 Towards fossilization
The shells of dead mussels are carried along and dropped together by water currents, where they are mixed with pebbles and sand to form "mussel beaches". Some mussels have two shells held together by tough tissue called ligament, but in others, this has broken and the shells have separated. The sea can break shells into small pieces. These may become buried and eventually fossilized.

Separated shell

Tough ligament holding shells together

Fossil mussel shell

5 Fossilized mussels
Small mussels can become embedded in rock. Here a natural mineral-cement binds the sediment grains and fossil shells together.

Blue fossils
The shells of living mussels are blue. Some colour remains in these fossil mussels, which are 2 million years old.

Lost colour
The colour in shells is usually lost during fossilization. The brown in these fossils is from the rock where they were fossilized.

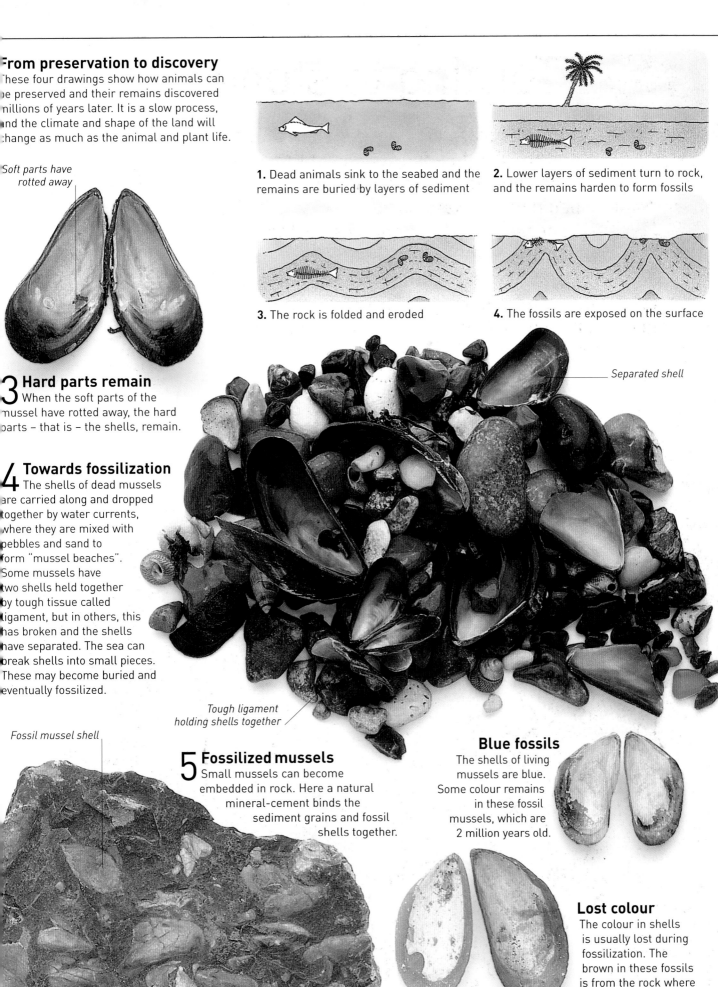

Changing World

Our planet has been changing since it formed about 4.6 billion years ago. Earth's crust is divided into different moving plates. Most earthquakes and volcanoes occur along boundaries between these plates. Small plate movements have caused continents to drift, to collide and form mountains, or to break into pieces. Sea levels and climates have changed many times. These maps show the land at four different stages in geological history. The fossils show examples of the life existing in each time span.

Continuous change
The earthquakes and volcanoes of recent times, such as the great earthquake of Lisbon, Portugal, in 1755, prove that changes are still taking place on Earth.

Old fossils
The oldest fossils are bacteria-like cells 3.5 billion years old. This Australian *Tribrachidium* appeared in the Precambrian time.

Silurian trilobites

Silurian graptolites

Silurian brachiopods

Silurian gastropod

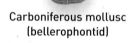
Carboniferous mollusc (bellerophontid)

Carboniferous coral

Devonian fish

Carboniferous seed fern

Carboniferous crinoid

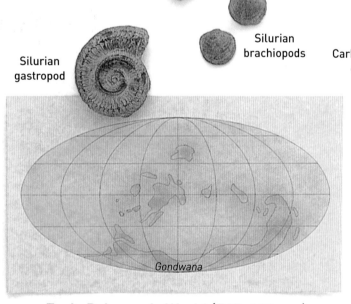
Gondwana

Early Palaeozoic World (545–418 MYA)
Palaeozoic means "ancient life". In the early Palaeozoic Era – Cambrian, Ordovician, and Silurian periods – a large continent, known as Gondwana, was situated over the southern polar region. Most early Palaeozoic life was in the sea.

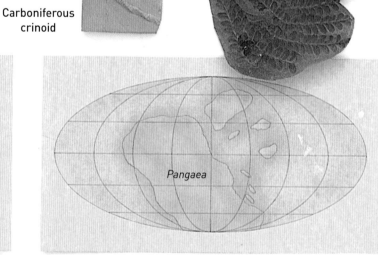
Pangaea

Late Palaeozoic World (417–249 MYA)
Life diversified in the late Palaeozoic Era (Devonian, Carboniferous, and Permian periods). Reptiles, insects, and other animals colonized the land. Most land became joined in one supercontinent, called Pangaea. A mass extinction occurred at the end of the era.

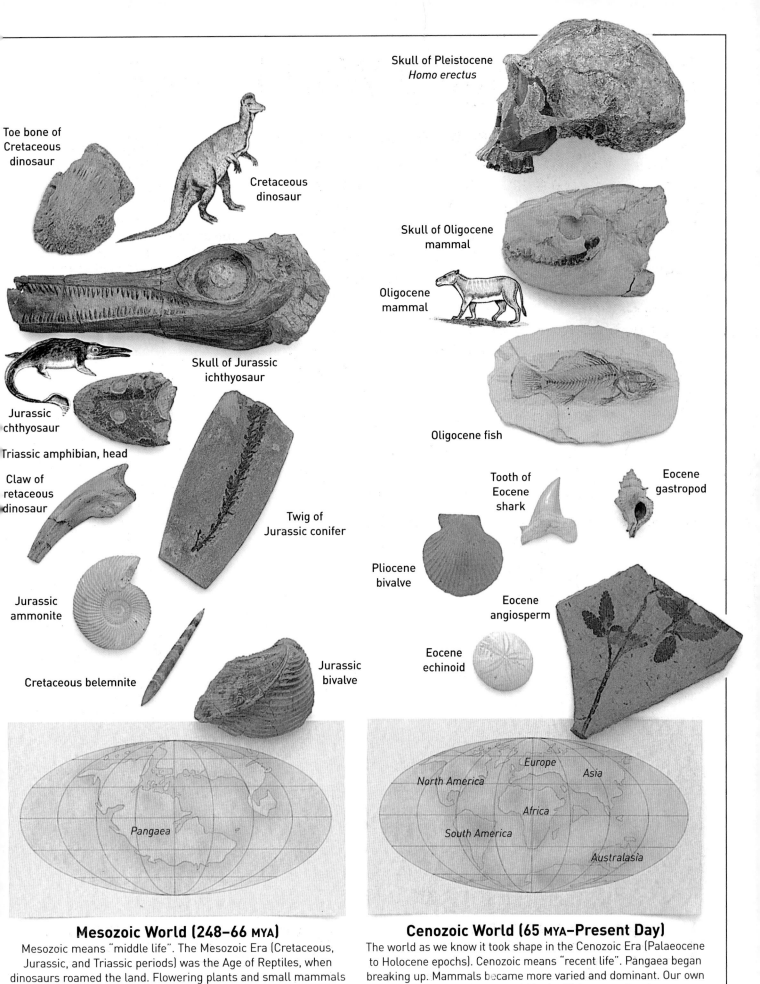

Skull of Pleistocene
Homo erectus

Toe bone of
Cretaceous
dinosaur

Cretaceous
dinosaur

Skull of Oligocene
mammal

Oligocene
mammal

Skull of Jurassic
ichthyosaur

Jurassic
ichthyosaur

Oligocene fish

Triassic amphibian, head

Claw of
Cretaceous
dinosaur

Tooth of
Eocene
shark

Eocene
gastropod

Twig of
Jurassic conifer

Pliocene
bivalve

Jurassic
ammonite

Eocene
angiosperm

Eocene
echinoid

Cretaceous belemnite

Jurassic
bivalve

Pangaea

Europe

Asia

North America

Africa

South America

Australasia

Mesozoic World (248–66 MYA)

Mesozoic means "middle life". The Mesozoic Era (Cretaceous,
Jurassic, and Triassic periods) was the Age of Reptiles, when
dinosaurs roamed the land. Flowering plants and small mammals
appeared. Many species died in another mass extinction.

Cenozoic World (65 MYA–Present Day)

The world as we know it took shape in the Cenozoic Era (Palaeocene
to Holocene epochs). Cenozoic means "recent life". Pangaea began
breaking up. Mammals became more varied and dominant. Our own
genus, *Homo*, appeared in the Pleistocene Epoch.

Early palaeontology

The scientific study of fossils began about 300 years ago, although early Greek philosophers are reported to have realized the true nature of fossils in the 5th century BCE. In the Middle Ages in Europe, many naturalists thought fossils were the products of a mysterious "plastic force" ("*vis plastica*") which formed the fossils within Earth. Their true origin as the buried remains of ancient animals and plants was established by 17th-century naturalists. Today's scientists are still studying fossils, and our understanding of them is increasing all the time.

This engraving shows naturalist Johann Scheuchzer (1672–1733).

Tongue stones
Fossil shark teeth from Cenozoic rocks around the Mediterranean, such as the ones above, were known to naturalists as "tongue stones".

Steno
Niels Stensen (1638–1686), known as Steno, was a Dane who worked as a court physician in Italy. He was one of the first people to realize the true nature of fossils, when in 1667 he noticed that the teeth of a stranded shark were similar to "tongue stones".

Noah's Ark
The Bible story of Noah tells how he took animals to his ark to escape the flood. Many naturalists thought this flood had taken and buried fossils. This explained why fossil seashells occurred on mountains.

Restoration
Cuvier studied *Palaeotherium* bones from the Eocene rocks of Paris. The animal from which they came was restored as this tapir-like mammal.

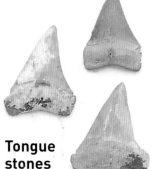

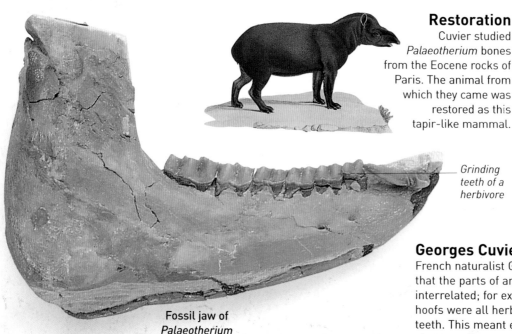

Fossil jaw of *Palaeotherium*

Grinding teeth of a herbivore

Georges Cuvier
French naturalist Georges Cuvier (1769–1832) realized that the parts of an animal's body were closely interrelated; for example, mammals with horns and hoofs were all herbivores and would have had herbivore teeth. This meant entire animals could be restored, shown as they would have looked when alive, from the evidence of isolated bones.

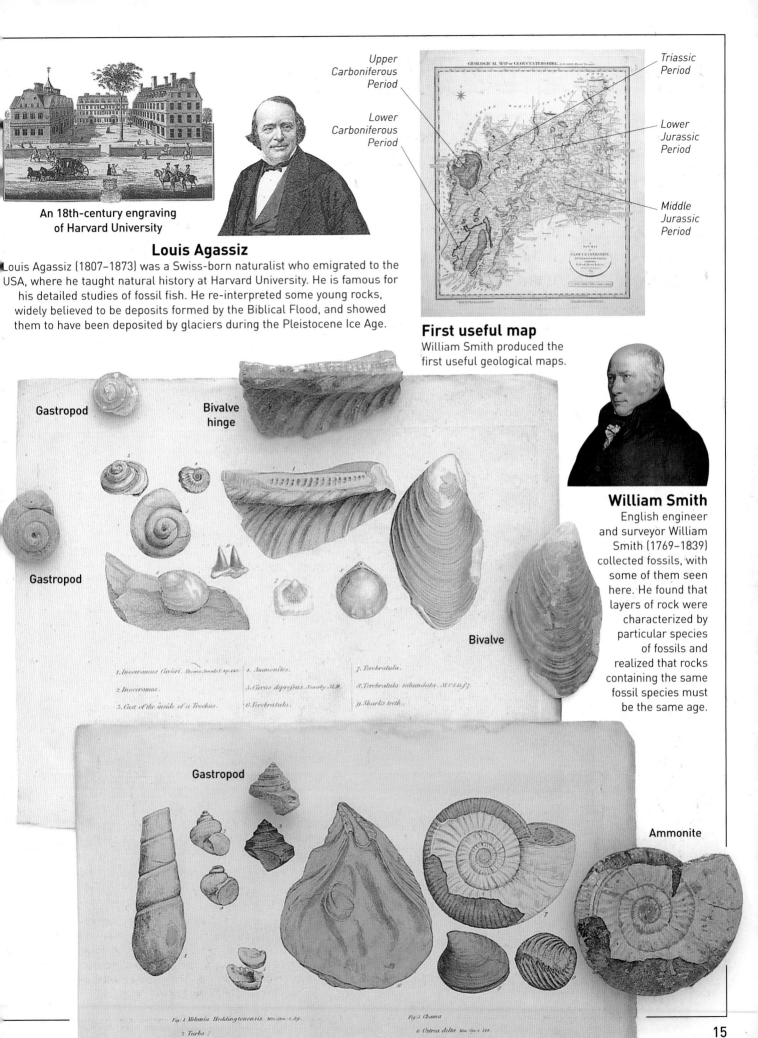

An 18th-century engraving
of Harvard University

Upper
Carboniferous
Period

Lower
Carboniferous
Period

Triassic
Period

Lower
Jurassic
Period

Middle
Jurassic
Period

Louis Agassiz

Louis Agassiz (1807–1873) was a Swiss-born naturalist who emigrated to the USA, where he taught natural history at Harvard University. He is famous for his detailed studies of fossil fish. He re-interpreted some young rocks, widely believed to be deposits formed by the Biblical Flood, and showed them to have been deposited by glaciers during the Pleistocene Ice Age.

First useful map
William Smith produced the first useful geological maps.

Gastropod

Bivalve
hinge

Gastropod

Gastropod

Bivalve

William Smith
English engineer and surveyor William Smith (1769–1839) collected fossils, with some of them seen here. He found that layers of rock were characterized by particular species of fossils and realized that rocks containing the same fossil species must be the same age.

1. Inoceramus Cuvieri. Thoma Annals V. 4p.448.   4. Ammonites.

2. Inoceramus.

3. Cast of the inside of a Trochus.   5. Cirrus depressus. Sowerby M.B.

6. Terebratula.

7. Terebratula.

8. Terebratula subundata. M.C.L5.f.7.

9. Sharks teeth.

Gastropod

Ammonite

Fig. 1 Melania Heddingtonensis. Min. Con. t. 39.

2 Turbo ?

Fig. 5 Chama

6 Ostrea delta Min. Con. t. 148.

7 Ammonites

Fossil folklore

Fossils are rich in folklore. For at least 10,000 years, fossils have featured in the beliefs, legends, and customs of ordinary people around the world. Even today, many people believe that particular types of fossils have supernatural or medicinal powers. Early people valued some fossils for their rarity or natural beauty. The origin of fossils was mysterious to people for a long time and led to some strange ideas about them.

Carved snake's head

Snakestone (ammonite)

Whitby coat of arms

Ancient Whitby coin

An artist's idea of the Devil

Devil's toenail

The Jurassic oyster *Gryphaea* had a thick curved shell, which is still known as a Devil's toenail. This explanation was given despite the fact that the Devil is usually described as having hoofs, not toes!

Snakestones

Ammonites from Whitby in England were said to be the remains of coiled snakes turned to stone by 7th-century abbess, St Hilda. Craftsmen carved heads on some ammonites. Three snakestones are shown in the Whitby coat of arms on this coin.

Thunderstones (fossil sea urchins)

Magic stones

Some people thought that fossil sea urchins were thunderstones fallen in a storm. One type was said to be hardened balls of froth made by snakes at midsummer. The snakes tossed them in the air and if one was caught in a cloth it had magical powers.

Toadstones

The shiny fossil teeth of the Mesozoic fish *Lepidotes* (see p.35) were said to come from toad heads. This woodcut from 1497 shows the removal of one.

Medicine

In the Middle Ages, toadstones were said to cure epilepsy and counter poison.

Woodcut from 1497

Old toad's tale

For medicinal purposes, toadstones were removed from the heads of old toads. These toads were meant to eject stones if placed on red cloth. In reality, toadstones have no connection with toads, but the name is used for fossil teeth of the extinct fish *Lepidotes*.

Toadstones (fossil fish teeth)

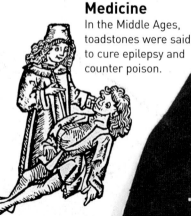

Famous myth
This French tapestry, called *The Lady and the Unicorn*, dates from 1500.

Unicornum verum (fossil mammoth tusk)

Real unicorn
The tusk of a small whale called the narwhal was identified for many years as the horn of the unicorn. However, the discovery in about 1600 of some fossil mammoth tusks led to these being proclaimed as the true horns of unicorns, or *unicornum verum*!

Lucky spines
This image shows the spines of sea urchin *Balanocidaris*, which were lucky charms in ancient times. They are found in Cretaceous rocks of an area in the Middle East once called Judea, hence their name Jewstones.

Natural hole through sponge

Porosphaera

Sponge beads
Bronze-Age people in Britain made necklaces by stringing together fossil sponges. Specimens of the Cretaceous sponge *Porosphaera* look like beads, and many have a hole in the middle.

Ancient burial
The skeletons of this woman clasping a child were found buried on Dunstable Down in England. Around the grave were three rows of fossil sea urchins, buried with them about 3,000 years ago, possibly to ward off evil spirits.

Thunderbolts (belemnites)

Stone swallow (fossil brachiopod)

Thunderbolts
The internal shells of extinct, squid-like animals called belemnites were said to have medicinal purposes. They were believed to fall as darts from the heavens during storms.

Take one shell
In China, the fossil shells of certain brachiopods are called Shiy-yen (stone swallows) and are still used as medicine. The prescription supplied with these Devonian brachiopods states they should be ground up, baked in a clay pot, and used as a cure for many illnesses.

京都 永仁堂

總 䰢 北 平 王 府 井 大 街 電 東 天 ...

石燕 甘 京

支 店 烟 台 北 大 街 電 話 四 百 六 十

主 赤 白 带 下

去 湿 止 淋

治 腸 風 痔 疾

眼 目 障 ...

Fossils of the future

The fossil record is a highly selective sample of ancient life. Many creatures did not have resistant hard parts and rotted away. Some lived where fossilization was unlikely to occur, such as the tree tops. Only a small proportion of life became fossilized. This selectivity is illustrated by looking at a modern community to see which animals and plants may become fossils in future.

Ray egg case

Cushion star

Brittlestar

Mackerels

Scallop

Scallop

Snail

Spiny starfish

Shrimps

Comm starfis

Sea mouse

Snail egg case

Bryozoan colony

Sponge

Temporary tenant

A good example of a creature that is unlikely to leave direct evidence of its existence is the hermit crab. Hermit crabs are unusual in having no shell of their own. They use old snail shells as homes. In some habitats, every available snail shell contains a hermit crab. Much of a hermit crab's body is soft and it twists in the spiral of the snail shell. The claws are hard, but are rarely fossilized because they decay and disintegrate.

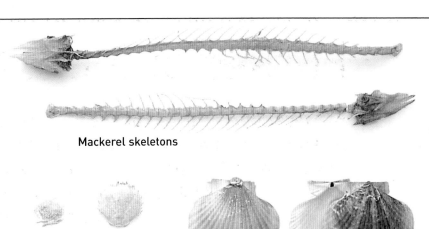

Mackerel skeletons

Dogfish teeth   Crab shell

Scallop shells

Green sea-urchin skeleton

Edible sea-urchin skeleton

Snail shell

Dogfish

The sample

Water communities are common in the fossil record because creatures that live in seas, lakes, and rivers are vulnerable to burial by mud or sand, which is often deposited in these environments. Most of this sample of animals and plants lived on the sea bed, though fish and shrimps swam in the water. Among the other animals are sea urchins, starfish, a brittlestar, scallops, a snail, a crab, a sponge, a sea mouse (worm), and bryozoan and hydroid colonies.

 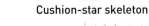

Common starfish skeleton

Cushion-star skeleton

Spiny starfish skeleton

The remains

The hard parts of animals are most likely to be fossilized, such as teeth, bones, and shells. The hard parts of the sample are shown here. Seaweeds and many animals have disappeared. All that remains of the dogfish are its teeth. A dogfish has a skeleton of non-resistant cartilage, not bone. Sea urchins, starfish, brittlestar, crab, and bryozoans had resistant skeletons, but these fell apart as the tissues connecting them decayed. Only the snail and scallop shells have hardly changed. This shows how little of a modern community would survive to be fossilized.

Brittlestar skeleton

Bryozoan skeletons

Edible sea urchin

Hydroid colony

Dogfish egg case

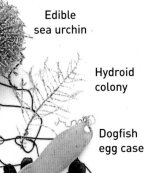

en a rchin

Crab

Leaving no trace

Animals and plants dying on land often decay before they can be fossilized. The fur and flesh of this reindeer carcass are rotting in the Arctic. The bones will disintegrate unless they are buried.

Remarkable remains

Occasionally, fossils of soft tissues, which usually decay during fossilization, are found. These include soft-bodied animals that are otherwise unrepresented in the fossil record. Fossilization of soft parts provides more information than bones, teeth, or shells.

Skin traces

In two parts
Traces of skin and tissue are preserved in this fossilized frog. The rock has split straight through the animal, leaving two pieces – the part and counterpart.

Part

Counterpart

Sticky end
A spider can be seen in this amber, the fossilized resin of an ancient plant. Amber often contains animals trapped in the sticky resin. Insects and frogs have been preserved for millions of years in this way.

Unique discovery
This unusual worm is from a deposit called the Burgess Shale in British Columbia, Canada, famous for its soft-bodied fossils. Other animals discovered in the Burgess Shale include trilobites and crustaceans. These animals were buried in mudflows on the Cambrian seabed over 500 million years ago.

Exceptional insect
This dragonfly is from the Solnhofen Limestone of West Germany.

Mammoth task
Mammoths have even been found in the permafrost (permanently frozen ground) of Siberia. They were probably trapped and frozen in glacier crevasses. Mammoths lived in the Ice Ages of the last 2 million years.

Active volcano
The famous volcano Vesuvius, in Italy, has erupted frequently. It has been quiet since 1944, but is not thought to be extinct.

Cast of body from Pompeii

Buried in ash
In the eruption of Mount Vesuvius in 79 CE, some inhabitants of the nearby towns of Pompeii and Herculaneum were buried beneath avalanches of volcanic ash. The ash hardened around the bodies and the bodies decayed, leaving cavities. The victims' bodies have been revealed by filling excavated cavities with plaster to give casts.

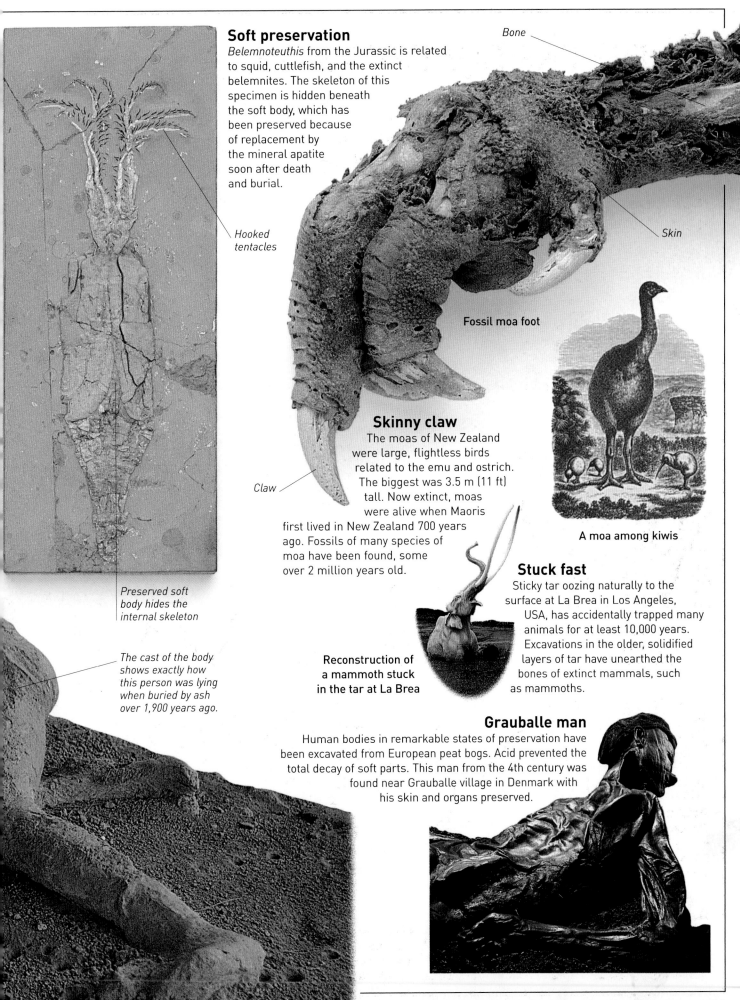

Soft preservation

Belemnoteuthis from the Jurassic is related to squid, cuttlefish, and the extinct belemnites. The skeleton of this specimen is hidden beneath the soft body, which has been preserved because of replacement by the mineral apatite soon after death and burial.

Hooked tentacles

Bone

Skin

Fossil moa foot

Preserved soft body hides the internal skeleton

The cast of the body shows exactly how this person was lying when buried by ash over 1,900 years ago.

Skinny claw

The moas of New Zealand were large, flightless birds related to the emu and ostrich. The biggest was 3.5 m (11 ft) tall. Now extinct, moas were alive when Maoris first lived in New Zealand 700 years ago. Fossils of many species of moa have been found, some over 2 million years old.

Claw

A moa among kiwis

Reconstruction of a mammoth stuck in the tar at La Brea

Stuck fast

Sticky tar oozing naturally to the surface at La Brea in Los Angeles, USA, has accidentally trapped many animals for at least 10,000 years. Excavations in the older, solidified layers of tar have unearthed the bones of extinct mammals, such as mammoths.

Grauballe man

Human bodies in remarkable states of preservation have been excavated from European peat bogs. Acid prevented the total decay of soft parts. This man from the 4th century was found near Grauballe village in Denmark with his skin and organs preserved.

Corals

The colourful massed tentacles of coral individuals, or polyps, resemble flowers in an undersea garden. Most corals live in tropical waters and feed on plankton. Corals may be solitary (living alone) or colonial (many polyps joined together). Fossil corals are common because beneath the soft-bodied polyps are hard, chalky skeletons.

Coral fishing
Coral has long been collected for its beauty and is used in jewellery.

A ring-shaped coral reef is called an atoll

Separate corallite

Corallite (individual coral skeleton)

Red limestone

Pipe coral
The pipe-shaped corallites (skeletons formed by individual polyps) of this Carboniferous coral colony, *Lithostrotion*, grew separately. Spaces between them are now filled with red limestone.

Horn coral
Aulophyllum is a solitary coral seen here in two parts. The pointed end was buried in seabed sediment, while soft polyp sat on the other end.

Crammed colony
This colonial coral, *Lonsdaleia*, belongs to the Rugosa group. Rugose corals became extinct in the Permian Period. Its corallites are many-sided and packed together.

Modern corals
Most modern corals belong to a group called the scleractinians, which first appeared in the Triassic Period. Coral reefs are the most diverse marine environments of all.

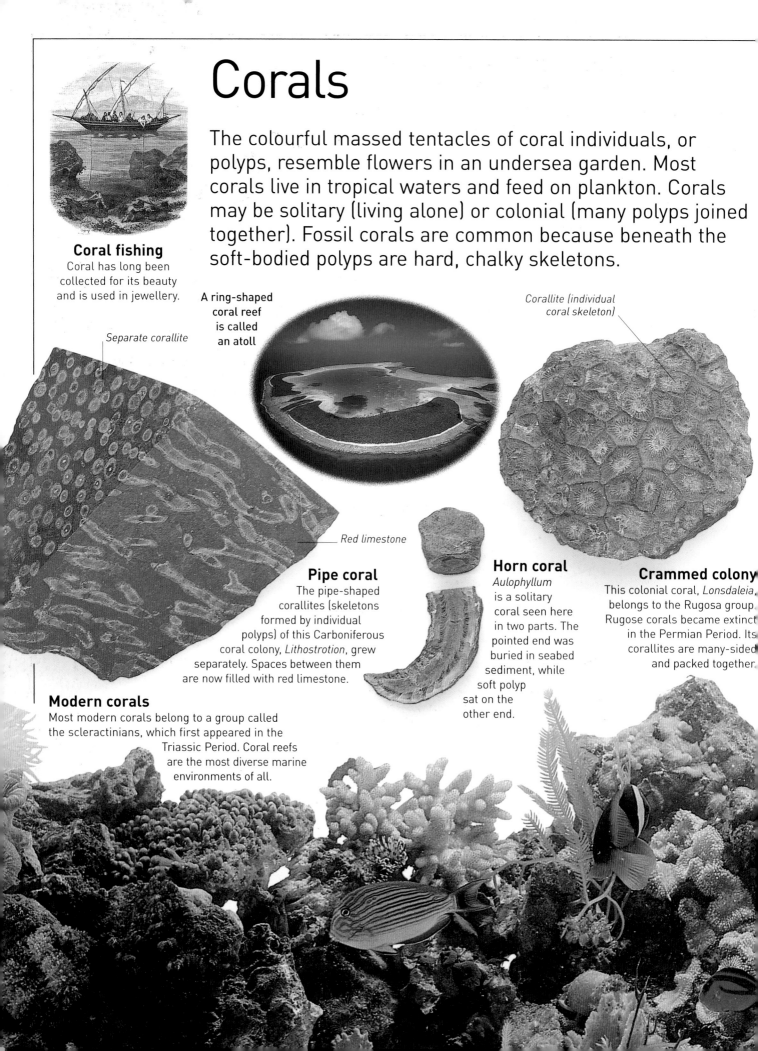

Chain coral

Pale sediment filling areas once occupied by soft tissues

This Silurian coral, *Halysites*, has corallites in branching ribbons. On the surface, it looks like a collection of chains.

Brain coral

Branch of corallites

Winding valley of coral

Together, the individuals of brain corals form winding valleys and the colonies resemble human brains. This Miocene example has been cut and polished.

Largest coral

This fossilized fragment of coral is the reef-building coral *Galaxea*. The world's largest-known living coral is a *Galaxea* colony from Okinawa in Japan, with a circumference of 16 m (52 ft).

Individual coral skeleton

Coral bush

Colonies of this coral, *Thamnopora*, are bush-shaped with corallites opening over the branches. This one in limestone has been cut horizontally and polished to show the colony shape.

Fossil *Fungia*

Solitary corals

These fossils are the skeletons of solitary corals *Stephanophyllia* and *Fungia*, which lived on the seabed in the Pliocene and Pleistocene periods respectively. The skeletons of *Fungia* look like the undersides of mushrooms.

Fossil *Stephanophyllia*

Replaced coral

Some fossil corals have skeletons made of the mineral aragonite. This dissolves easily, so the skeletons often disappear in fossilization. In this fossil colony of *Thecosmilia*, the skeletons have been replaced by silica.

Skeleton replaced by silica

Seabed dwellers

The most common fossils are the animal and plant remains on the seabed. They lived where sand and mud was deposited, and most had hard parts that could survive decay and be fossilized. Plants and many animals were buried because they did not move. Bryozoans and brachiopods are living examples. There are 250 known species of brachiopods today, but 30,000 known fossil species.

Close neighbours
Bryozoan colonies can be compared to blocks of flats and other buildings containing several similar homes.

Holes in the colony through which water and food particles are pumped

Archimedes' screw
This distinctive Carboniferous bryozoan is named after a spiral water pump invented by Greek philosopher Archimedes because of its screw-shaped skeleton.

Archimedes' water pump

Each piece is a colony containing at least 200 individuals

Free-living colonies of Cretaceous bryozoans

Community homes
The branching shape of this modern bryozoan, *Hornera*, provides a home for worms, fishes, and other marine life.

Individual skeleton

Larger than life
A bryozoan colony is shown magnified here.

Calcite colonies

Bryozoans are tiny animals that live in colonies in which each individual is attached to its neighbour. A colony may house thousands of individuals, each one less than 1 mm (0.04 in) long. They have tentacles to feed on tiny pieces of food. Most have skeletons made of calcite. Some colonies are flat sheets, while others grow upright.

Light and dark growth bands

Old lace
Lace bryozoan (*Chasmatopora*) in this Ordovician shale are among the oldest known bryozoans.

Red stone
The red of this Jurassic alga, *Solenopora*, can be preserved. These fossils are known as beetroot stones.

Shells on stalks

Brachiopods have two shells and can be mistaken for bivalve molluscs. A brachiopod shell is symmetrical, but one is larger than the other. A bivalve shell is asymmetrical in shape, but is a mirror image of its pair. The soft parts of bivalve molluscs are also different.

Hole for stalk

Fossil brachiopod

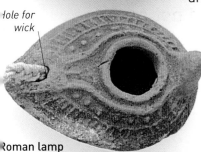

Hole for wick

Roman lamp

Lamp shells

Brachiopods are called lamp shells because they are similar to ancient Roman lamps. The hole at one end of the lamp for a wick is like the hole in the brachiopod shell for its stalk.

Spiriferid brachiopods

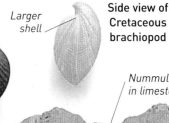

Winged shells

Spiriferid brachiopods had an internal spiral-shaped feeding organ, supported by a skeleton.

Hole for stalk

Symmetrical shell

Modern brachiopods

Today's colour

These red brachiopods of today are similar to the Cretaceous one that has lost any colour it might have had during fossilization.

Larger shell

Side view of Cretaceous brachiopod

Nummulite skeleton in limestone

Pyramid skeletons

The Pyramids of Giza in Egypt are built of limestone blocks made up of skeletons such as *Nummulites*.

Polished fossil *Siphonia* sponge

Modern branching sponge

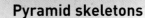

Sponges

Sponges are a primitive group of animals that pump water through their bodies. Sponge skeletons have small spicules, which can often be fossilized. Fossil sponges first occurred in the Cambrian Period.

Fossil tulip sponge

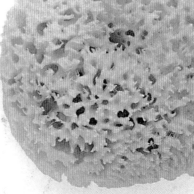

Pyramids of Ancient Egypt

Skeleton cup

Skeletons of sponges with fused spicules can be preserved. Many are cup-shaped like this Cretaceous example.

Sponge skeleton treated to make a bath sponge

Shell shapes

At the start of the Cambrian Period, about 545 million years ago, complex animals with hard shells and skeletons appeared in the sea. Among them were molluscs, a group still abundant today. Gastropods, or snails, and bivalves such as mussels, clams, and oysters are the most familiar molluscs, but others include chitons and cephalopods. The calcite or aragonite shells of molluscs are often found as fossils.

Venus's shell
The goddess Venus depicted emerging from a scallop shell

Pearl

Ancient jewels
This mudstone contains rare fossil pearls.

Muscle scar

Hinge tooth

Hinged together
Hinge teeth helped hold a bivalve's shells together. This was from an Eocene bivalve, *Venericardia*.

Shell — *Eye* — *Gape*

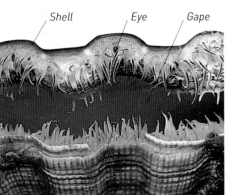

Sensory tentacles

Good eyesight
Scallops have many eyes, each with well-developed lenses. They sit in soft tissue by the shell edge. Scallop shells are hinged together. To feed, they use their gills to cause a current of water laden with food particles to pass through the shell gape.

Spiny sponges
The "thorny oyster" *Spondylus* is named for its spiny shell, as seen here in this Pliocene specimen.

Prominent rib

Fall apart
These fossilized shells belong to the scallop *Pecten*, from the Pliocene Epoch. The ribs on the two shells interlock, but the shells often separate as ligament decomposes.

Carved in stone
These fossils are carved with an Arabic prayer. They are casts of bivalves, formed by sediment between the shells.

Modern cone shell

Fossil cone shell

Modern snail shell

Fossil snail shells

Disappearing colour

Some living gastropods, especially those of the tropics, are often brightly coloured. Their colour is due to pigment, a chemical substance within the shell. Pigments are usually destroyed during fossilization, as seen in the examples above.

\ *Siphon*

― *Foot*

Soft-hearted

This modern sea snail is just emerging from its shell. Parts of its soft body can be seen (at top and bottom right).

Modern snail

Curious coils

Gastropod shells of all ages come in different shapes and sizes. They are all open at one end with an increasing diameter and are usually twisted into a spiral coil. The spiral shape can be left-handed, right-handed, loosely coiled, or tightly coiled. *Turritella* has a shell which is drawn out into a high spire.

― *Spiral coil*

Fossil *Turritella*

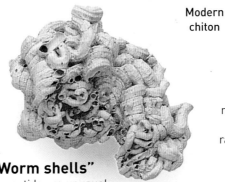

"Worm shells"

Vermetids are unusual gastropods as they attach themselves to a hard surface, often in clusters like these fossils. Their shells look like worms.

Fossil chiton

Modern chiton

No connection

Chitons are a small group of marine molluscs with shells made up of eight individual plates. Fossil chitons are rare and their plates are disconnected. Today chitons can be found in rock pools, sticking to the rocks from which they scrape algae for food.

Loose coils

Tubina is a mollusc belonging to an extinct group, the bellerophontids. It has a loosely coiled shell and dates back to the Devonian Period.

Fossil
Neptunea
contraria

― *Left-handed coil*

― *Right-handed coil*

Fossil
Neptunea
despecta

― *Siphonal canal*

Right or left

Most gastropods have shells with a right-handed spiral coil, such as *Neptunea despecta*.

Extra long

The *Fusinus* shell has a siphonal canal used in respiration.

Top

Underneath

Fossil *Planorbis*

An ammonite with its shell partly replaced by iron pyrites

Mighty molluscs

The octopus, squid, and cuttlefish are modern representatives of a group of sea-dwelling molluscs called cephalopods, which have left a rich fossil record. They are the most highly developed molluscs, with suckered tentacles, advanced eyes, and the ability to learn. They are active predators, moving quickly through the water using jet propulsion. Following their first appearance in the Cambrian Period, many species came and went, making them useful fossils for dating rocks.

Ammonite art

Ammonites are used in decoration. This column is from a house in Brighton, England. The architect was named Amon!

Important evidence

As the only living Nautiloid, *Nautilus* is the closest relative of the ammonites, and provides information about this extinct group. *Nautilus* is a nocturnal animal, active at night, and lives in the Pacific Ocean at depths up to 550 m (1,800 ft). It eats fish and crustaceans.

Septa dividing shell into chambers

Final chamber

Complex suture line

Ammonites

Various sizes

Some Mesozoic ammonites reached gigantic sizes. This large specimen, 30 cm (12 in) wide, is small compared to giants that could be 2 m (6 ft 6 in) in diameter.

Simple suture line

Fossil nautiloids

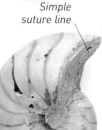

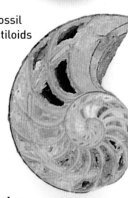

Rooms for expansion

Fossil ammonites and nautiloids have coiled shells divided into chambers by septa. Only the last chamber was occupied by the animal. As it grew, the animal moved forwards and formed new septa. Older chambers filled with liquid and gas to let the animal move up and down in the sea. Suture lines where the septa meet the shell are simple in nautiloids but complex in ammonites.

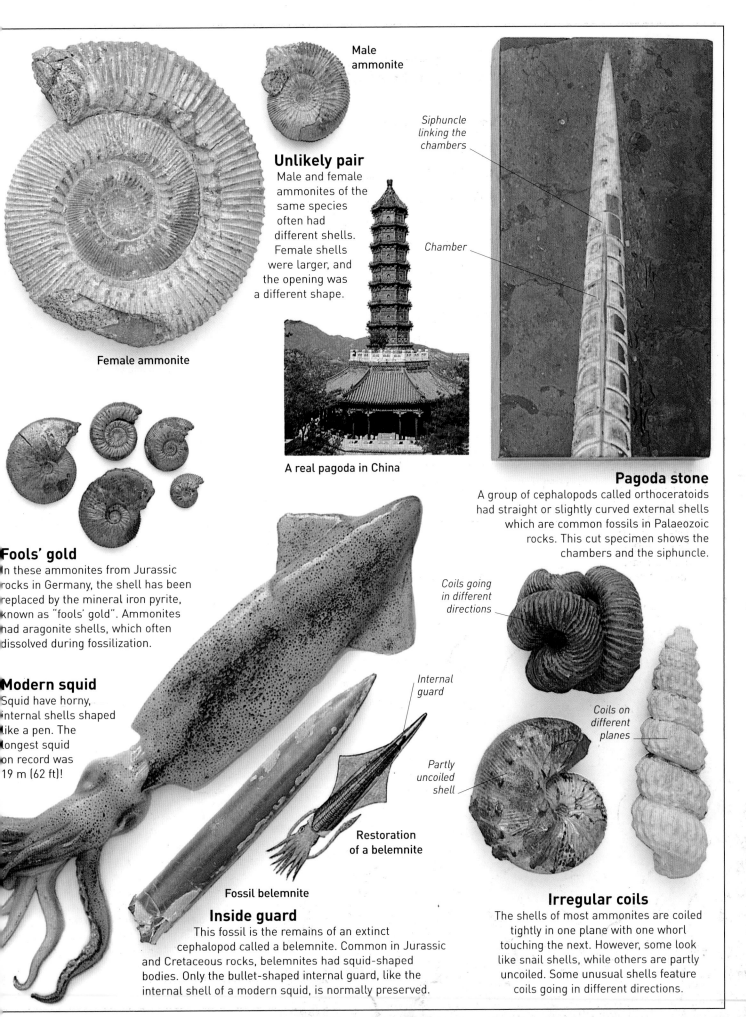

Female ammonite

Male ammonite

Unlikely pair

Male and female ammonites of the same species often had different shells. Female shells were larger, and the opening was a different shape.

A real pagoda in China

Siphuncle linking the chambers

Chamber

Pagoda stone

A group of cephalopods called orthoceratoids had straight or slightly curved external shells which are common fossils in Palaeozoic rocks. This cut specimen shows the chambers and the siphuncle.

Fools' gold

In these ammonites from Jurassic rocks in Germany, the shell has been replaced by the mineral iron pyrite, known as "fools' gold". Ammonites had aragonite shells, which often dissolved during fossilization.

Modern squid

Squid have horny, internal shells shaped like a pen. The longest squid on record was 19 m (62 ft)!

Internal guard

Partly uncoiled shell

Coils going in different directions

Coils on different planes

Restoration of a belemnite

Fossil belemnite

Inside guard

This fossil is the remains of an extinct cephalopod called a belemnite. Common in Jurassic and Cretaceous rocks, belemnites had squid-shaped bodies. Only the bullet-shaped internal guard, like the internal shell of a modern squid, is normally preserved.

Irregular coils

The shells of most ammonites are coiled tightly in one plane with one whorl touching the next. However, some look like snail shells, while others are partly uncoiled. Some unusual shells feature coils going in different directions.

Animals in armour

Insects, spiders, crabs, scorpions, and lobsters belong to a large group of animals called arthropods, meaning "jointed foot". They have jointed legs, a segmented body, and an exoskeleton, or outer armour. Some arthropods, such as the extinct trilobites, have the mineral calcite in their exoskeletons, which makes them resist decay. These exoskeletons are often found fossilized.

Prize piece
Trilobites are prize fossils. This Siluria Calymene has been m into a brooch. This spe was found in Dudle England, and nicknam the Dudley bug.

Small is beautiful
Most trilobites were 3–10 cm (1–4 in) long. These ones are *Elrathia*.

Eye

No eyes

Trilobite *Dalmanites*

Trilobite *Concoryphe*

To see or not to see?
More than 10,000 species of trilobites once lived in the sea. Some swam and floated, while other crawled on the seabed. Most species had two eyes and good vision. Lenses can be preserved in fossil trilobites because of the resistant mineral calcite. Some species in the deep sea had no eyes.

Modern millipede

Fossil millipede

Early settlers
Like all arthropods, millipedes have bodies divided into pieces, or segments. They were one of the first animals on land.

Packed lenses

Multi-vision
Trilobite eyes are the most ancient visual systems known. Each tiny lens produced its own image.

Echinocaris, a Devonian shrimp-like arthropod

Roll up!
Some trilobites could roll up like woodlice, probably for protection against predators.

Long spine

Tri-lobed
The name trilobite came from the exoskeletons divided into three parts or lobes. Whole fossil trilobites can be found in rocks from the Cambrian to the Permian Period, about 545 to 248 million years old. *Paradoxides* from the Cambrian Period grew to 50 cm (1 ft 7 in) long.

Prickly customer
This Devonian trilobite, *Dicranurus*, was notable for its long spines.

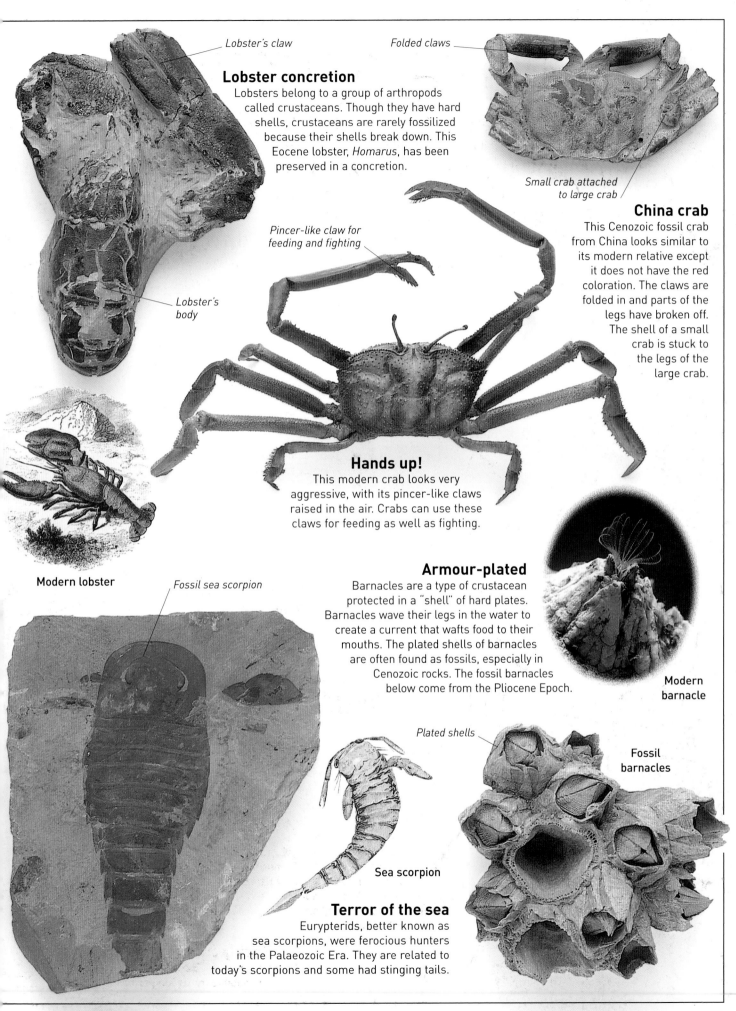

Lobster concretion

Lobster's claw

Lobsters belong to a group of arthropods called crustaceans. Though they have hard shells, crustaceans are rarely fossilized because their shells break down. This Eocene lobster, *Homarus*, has been preserved in a concretion.

Lobster's body

Folded claws

Small crab attached to large crab

China crab

This Cenozoic fossil crab from China looks similar to its modern relative except it does not have the red coloration. The claws are folded in and parts of the legs have broken off. The shell of a small crab is stuck to the legs of the large crab.

Pincer-like claw for feeding and fighting

Hands up!

This modern crab looks very aggressive, with its pincer-like claws raised in the air. Crabs can use these claws for feeding as well as fighting.

Modern lobster

Armour-plated

Barnacles are a type of crustacean protected in a "shell" of hard plates. Barnacles wave their legs in the water to create a current that wafts food to their mouths. The plated shells of barnacles are often found as fossils, especially in Cenozoic rocks. The fossil barnacles below come from the Pliocene Epoch.

Modern barnacle

Fossil sea scorpion

Plated shells

Fossil barnacles

Sea scorpion

Terror of the sea

Eurypterids, better known as sea scorpions, were ferocious hunters in the Palaeozoic Era. They are related to today's scorpions and some had stinging tails.

Arms and spines

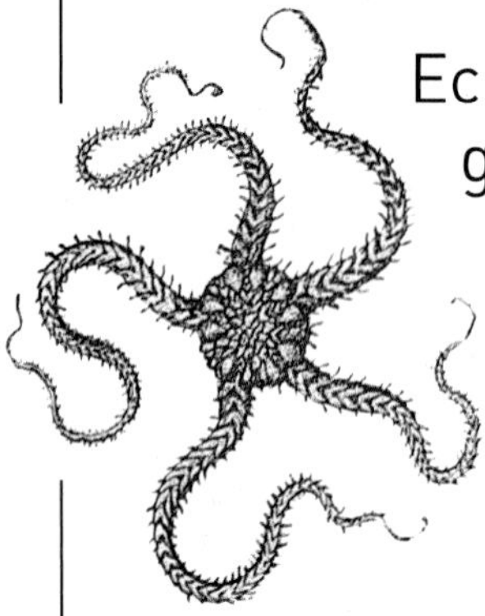

Echinoderms are a distinctive group of sea creatures, including sea urchins (echinoids), sea lilies (crinoids), starfish (asteroids), and brittlestars (ophiuroids). Most echinoderms have five-fold radial symmetry, meaning their bodies can be divided into five similar segments. As echinoderms have skeletons made of resistant calcite, they are often found fossilized.

Modern brittlestar

Interlinked delicate arms

Arm in arm
This Jurassic specimen shows a group of five fossil brittlestars with interlinking arms. Brittlestars look like starfish, but their arms break off easily – hence their name. They use their arms to move across the seabed.

Symmetrical arm

Modern *Protoreaster*

Star hunter
Many starfish are efficient hunters, often feeding on bivalves, which they open using arm suckers. Others, like this Australian *Protoreaster*, extract food from sediments such as sand.

Star of the beach
Starfish can be found in rock pools and beaches by the sea, but they are rarely found as fossils.

Mouth

Ammonite

Mouth

Underside of modern starfish

Suckers

Position of missing arm

Arm robbery
This fossil starfish from the Jurassic, seen from underneath, is similar to modern species, but an arm is missing. Its mouth is in the centre. The rock contains tiny ammonites and shell fragments.

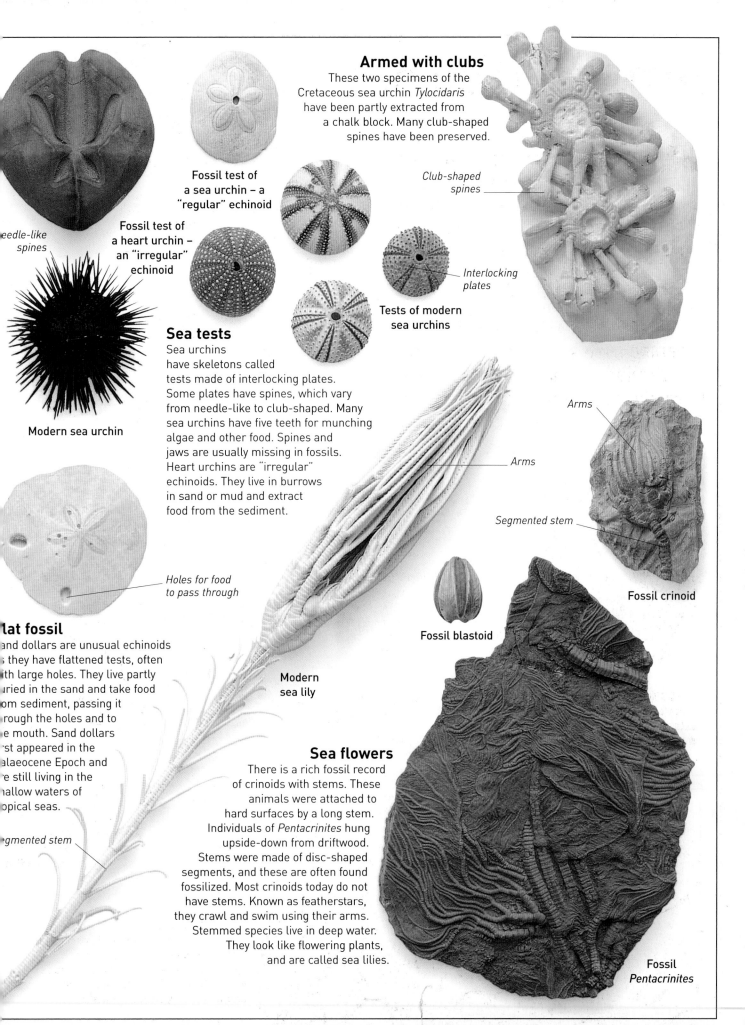

Armed with clubs

These two specimens of the Cretaceous sea urchin *Tylocidaris* have been partly extracted from a chalk block. Many club-shaped spines have been preserved.

Club-shaped spines

needle-like spines

Fossil test of a sea urchin – a "regular" echinoid

Fossil test of a heart urchin – an "irregular" echinoid

Interlocking plates

Tests of modern sea urchins

Modern sea urchin

Sea tests

Sea urchins have skeletons called tests made of interlocking plates. Some plates have spines, which vary from needle-like to club-shaped. Many sea urchins have five teeth for munching algae and other food. Spines and jaws are usually missing in fossils. Heart urchins are "irregular" echinoids. They live in burrows in sand or mud and extract food from the sediment.

Arms

Arms

Fossil crinoid

Segmented stem

Holes for food to pass through

lat fossil

and dollars are unusual echinoids
s they have flattened tests, often
th large holes. They live partly
ried in the sand and take food
om sediment, passing it
rough the holes and to
e mouth. Sand dollars
st appeared in the
alaeocene Epoch and
e still living in the
allow waters of
opical seas.

gmented stem

Modern sea lily

Fossil blastoid

Sea flowers

There is a rich fossil record of crinoids with stems. These animals were attached to hard surfaces by a long stem. Individuals of *Pentacrinites* hung upside-down from driftwood. Stems were made of disc-shaped segments, and these are often found fossilized. Most crinoids today do not have stems. Known as featherstars, they crawl and swim using their arms. Stemmed species live in deep water. They look like flowering plants, and are called sea lilies.

Fossil *Pentacrinites*

Fish

Fish are the most primitive vertebrates (animals with backbones). They have gills to breathe and fins to swim. There are 20,000 species. Fish appeared about 500 million years ago. Most were small, jawless, and covered in armour. In the Devonian Period, called the Age of Fish, fish became plentiful. Skeletons of fossil fish are found in specific areas, but it is more common to discover teeth.

Sparnodus part

Shark spine

Sharks and rays have soft cartilage skeletons, which are not normally fossilized. They have resistant teeth and spines, with fossils dating to the Devonian Period.

Jurassic shark spine

Dorsal fin

Impression of a modern shark

Sharp teeth

Jaws

One of the first known fish with jaws was a group of armoured fish called placoderms.

Teeth of an Eocene sand shark, *Eugomphodus*

Shark teeth

Most sharks are fierce predators with sharp teeth. The largest recorded modern shark was a great white measuring 9 m (30 ft). However, its extinct relative, *Carcharodon*, had a tooth of 11 cm (4 in), suggesting a body length of 12 m (39 ft).

Modern ray

Tooth of Pliocene shark, *Carcharadon*

Ptychodus tooth

Ridges for crushing food

Ridged Ptychodu tooth

Jawless fish

Cephalaspids were primitive freshwater fish. They were jawless and fed by sucking sediment.

Shell crushers

Fossil teeth are all that is known of a cartilaginous fish, *Ptychodus*, which was like a modern ray. Its ridged teeth crushed up mollusc shells.

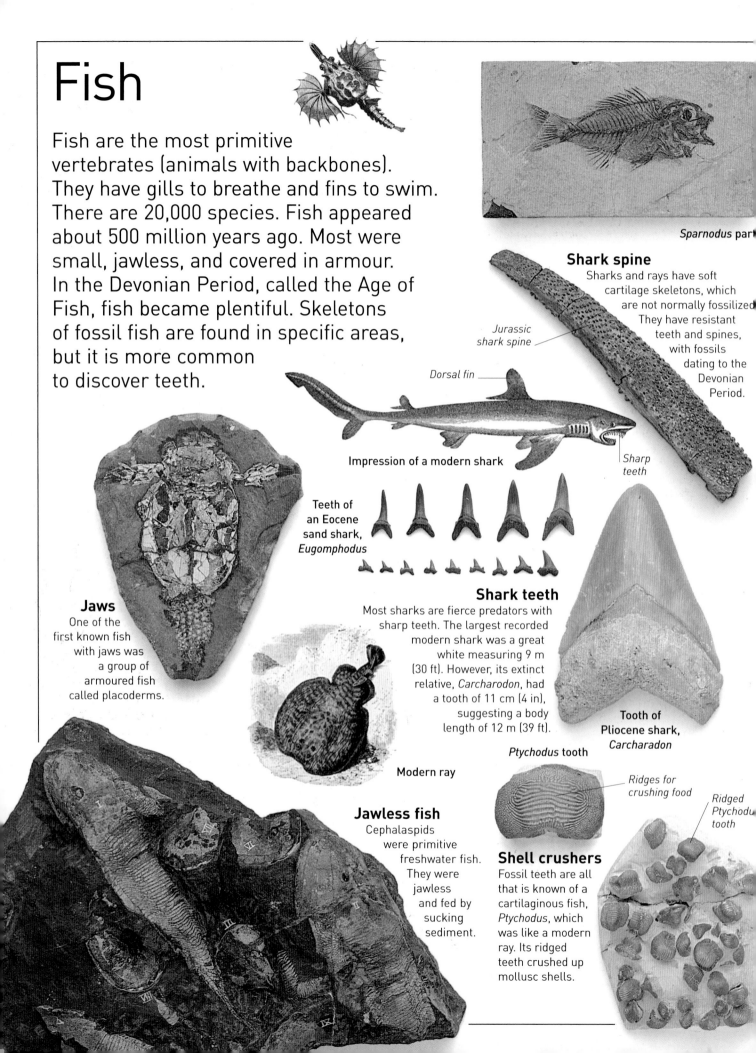

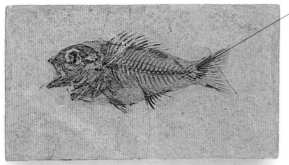
Well-preserved skeleton

Sparnodus counterpart

Fish eats fish
Fossils rarely provide evidence of an animal's diet. However this Cretaceous dogfish contains a teleost head that it swallowed. The dogfish had tiny teeth, so it probably scavenged the head from a fish that was already dead.

Swallowed fish head

Two parts
This slab of Eocene limestone has split through a fossil specimen of Sparnodus. The two bits are the part and the counterpart. Sparnodus belongs to a group of bony fish alive today called porgies or sea breams.

Thick-scaled fish
epidotes was a Mesozoic bony fish. It was found all over the world and some grew to almost 2 m (6 ft 6 in). The body was covered in thick scales.

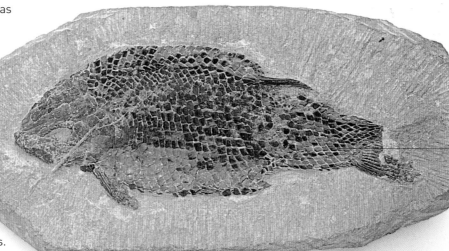
Scales covering the body

Ear stones
Otoliths are balance organs from the ears of fish. They are made of chalky material and form unusual fossils. These examples are from Eocene fish.

Sharp predator's teeth

Modern African lungfish

Teeth for hunting
From the Jurassic, *Caturus* had sharp teeth.

Armoured head

Thick scales

Bony fish
About 200 million years ago, this primitive teleost, a type of bony fish, lived in the seas. Teleosts appeared in the Triassic, and today they are the most common type of fish. They include carp, salmon, cod, and mackerel.

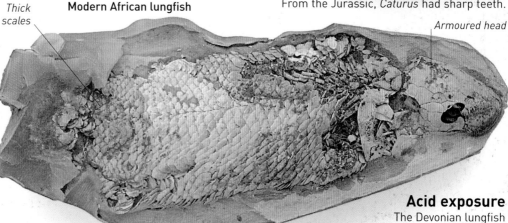
Remains of concretion

Acid exposure
The Devonian lungfish *Chirodipterus* had thick, bony scales. This Australian specimen was preserved in a chalky concretion and has been exposed by acid treatment, which dissolved the concretion but not the fish.

Plant pioneers

The invasion of the land by plants about 440 million years ago was a key event in the history of life. It paved the way for colonization by animals and was the starting point for the plants we see today. Plants on land had to support themselves against gravity, be resistant to drying, and transport water from the roots to the higher plant, where energy-producing photosynthesis occurred. These adaptations were first seen in primitive land plants of the Palaeozoic Era.

Jet jewels
Jet is a fossil wood dense enough to carve and polish for jewellery. Jet formed when wood from monkey puzzle trees was washed into the sea.

Impression in sandstone of the bark of *Lepidodendron*

Diamond-shaped leaf-scars

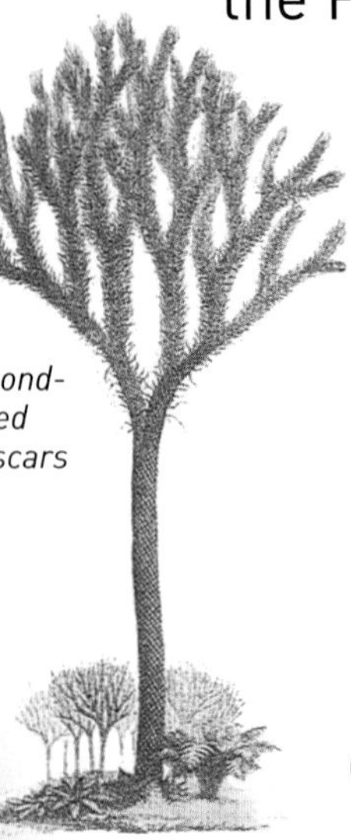

Lepidodendron

Cross-section of the fossil cone *Lepidostrobus*

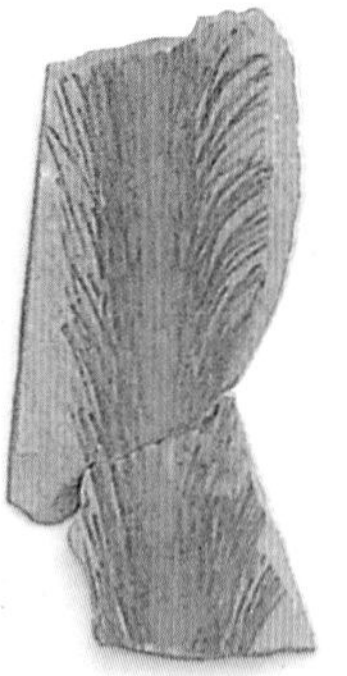

Johann Scheuchzer
Swiss naturalist Johann Scheuchzer (1672–1733) studied fossil plants and fish from the Miocene rocks in Switzerland.

Clubmosses

Clubmosses, belonging to a plant group called lycopods, reproduce by spores held in cones. Lycopods were common in the Palaeozoic Era. *Baragwanathia* from the Devonian of Australia is the oldest example. Palaeozoic lycopods grew as trees, with *Lepidodendron* stretching 40 m (130 ft).

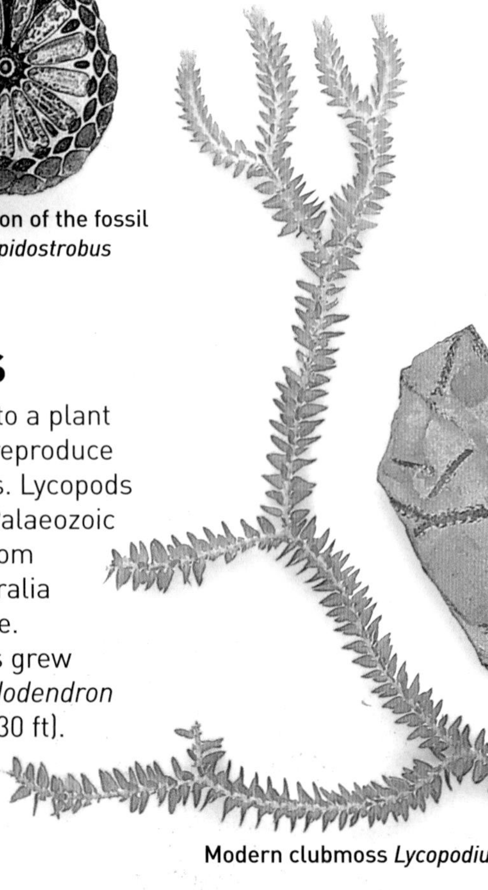

Fossil Baragwanathia

Carboniferous clubmoss *Archaeosigillar*

Modern clubmoss *Lycopodium*

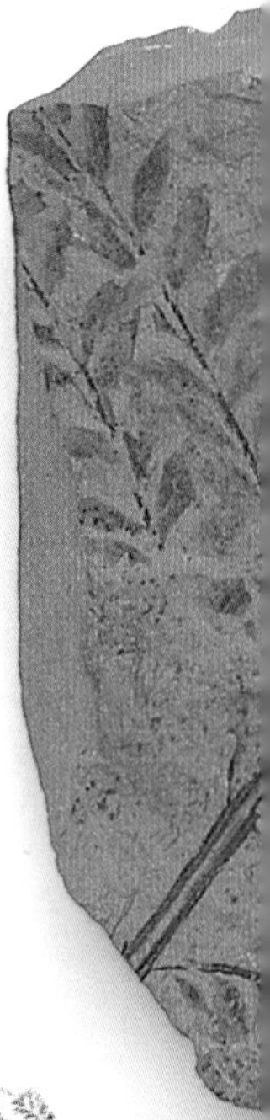

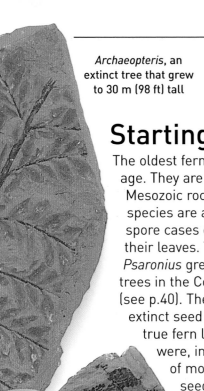

Archaeopteris, an extinct tree that grew to 30 m (98 ft) tall

Starting seeds

The oldest ferns are of Devonian age. They are common fossils in Mesozoic rocks and about 10,000 species are alive today. They have spore cases on the underside of their leaves. Tree ferns such as *Psaronius* grew alongside clubmoss trees in the Coal Measure forests (see p.40). The leaves of the now-extinct seed ferns resemble true fern leaves, but they were, in fact, relatives of more advanced, seed-bearing plants.

Modern fern

Compressed fern

Carbonized leaves of Jurassic fern *Coniopteris*, preserved, as compressions.

Plants in a typical Palaeozoic scene

Familiar fern

Iodites from the Jurassic is a typical fern – the fronds are similar to modern species.

Polished fern

This piece of fossil wood is from tree fern *Psaronius*, which reached 8 m (26 ft).

This image shows the only modern horsetail genus, *Equisetum*, which grows to 1.5 m (5 ft) tall

Fossil cones

This fossil monkey puzzle cone has been sectioned to show the internal structure.

Seed spread

The presence of fossils of this seed fern, *Glossopteris*, in India, Africa, South America, Australia, and Antarctica, prove these areas were once linked as Gondwana.

Leathery leaf

Monkey puzzle

The monkey puzzle is a primitive conifer that appeared in the Triassic. Today it grows in the Andes mountains in South America.

Modern monkey puzzle branch

Horsetails

Horsetails date from the Devonian, reaching 18 m (60 ft). This is a Jurassic *Equisetites* stem.

Leaf-bearing part of stem

Equisetites

Underground part of stem

Continued on next page

Protected seeds

Most modern seed-producing plants have their seeds protected in a fruit (flowering plants, or angiosperms) or a cone (gymnosperms, including conifers). Angiosperms are the most successful modern plants. There are about 250,000 species compared with 50,000 species of other plants. Angiosperms include grasses, oaks, tulips, palms, potatoes, and cacti. They appear late in the fossil record. The earliest examples come from the Cretaceous Period. The earliest conifer fossils occur earlier in the Carboniferous Period.

Fossil cycad

Palm-like leaf

Soft fruit
All fruits contain seeds. Soft fruits decay quickly. Hard seeds are more likely to be fossilized.

Before flowers
When angiosperms first appeared, cycads were common plants. These palm-like gymnosperms produced seeds in separate cone-like structures. Modern cycads still look like palms, and nine types live in tropical forests.

Cycad companion
Other gymnosperms were also living at this time, and some Cretaceous conifer wood has been petrified (turned to stone). This has preserved details of the original wood.

Annual rings preserved in stone

Sabal leaf

Petrified conifer wood

Fossil palm
There are two main types of angiosperms – monocotyledons and dicotyledons. Generally, monocotyledons have leaves with parallel veins, while dicotyledons have net-veined leaves. Palms, like this *Sabal* from the Eocene, and grasses are monocotyledons. All other angiosperms shown are dicotyledons.

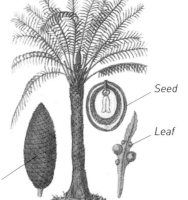

Palm-like tree

Seed

Leaf

"Cone"

Modern cycad

Split in two
Angiosperm leaves are well-preserved in some fine-grained sedimentary rocks. This Miocene example of a myrtle leaf has been fractured into two parts.

Leaf of a modern palm

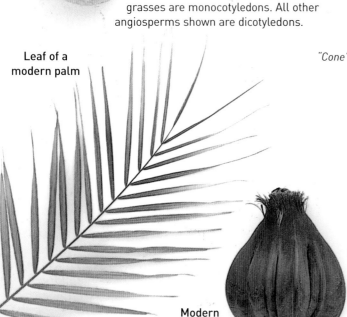

Fossil *Nipa* fruit

Coast guards
A fruit of a modern *Nipa* tree is compared here with a smaller fossil *Nipa* fruit from the Eocene. *Nipa* is a stemless palm that grows along tropical coastlines.

Modern *Nipa* fruit

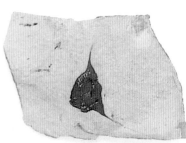

Flat chestnut
This is the flattened seed of a water chestnut from the Miocene Epoch.

Modern poplar leaves

Juglans seeds

Palliopora seeds

Tectocarya seeds

Small change
Fossil poplar leaves are almost identical to poplars today. This one is about 25 million years old. Modern poplar trees can grow to 40 m (130 ft) tall.

Fossil poplar leaf

Mastixia seeds

Greatly magnified fossil pollen

Ancient seeds
Angiosperm seeds are often enclosed in a fleshy fruit that animals eat before the seeds are dispersed. Various types of fossil fruits and seeds are common from the Late Cretaceous Period onwards.

First pollen
This Cretaceous pollen grain is an early angiosperm pollen.

Giant conifer
Giant redwoods are conifers now in North America. Conifers are gymnosperms and produce seeds inside cones. Fossils include rooted stumps, cones, and seeds.

Fossil Miocene leaves

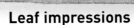

Fossil maple leaf showing midrib and veins

Leaf impressions
These Miocene leaves are preserved as impressions in limestone. The three-lobed leaf with midrib and delicate veins is a maple.

Leaves of a modern maple

Bud

In bud
Buds are rarely preserved in fossil plants, but one is attached to this Miocene maple tree.

Stone rings
Growth rings, like those in the wood of trees today, show in this section of petrified oak wood. They give information about the tree's growth and the climate when the tree was living.

Growth rings

Preserved petals
Fossils of flowers are seldom found, so these petals of *Porana* from the Miocene Epoch are exceptional. A flower today with similar petals is the primrose.

Fossil flower

Modern primrose

Fossil fuels

Oil and coal are called fossil fuels because they originate from ancient organisms, mainly plants. When burned, they release energy, in the form of heat and light, that was originally captured by living plants during photosynthesis millions of years ago. Fossil fuels are extracted from Earth in huge quantities.

Living mosses and grasses

Peat
These plants will die and add their remains to the peat. Dried peat can be a fuel for household fires.

A Coal Measure forest

Coal plant
This impression of bark is of a plant from the Coal Measure forests of the Carboniferous Period. About two-thirds of the world's coal supply came from these plants.

Crack caused when drying

Lignite
The first stage of coal formation may still contain water. It crumbles easily and may crack as it dries in the air.

From plant to coal

Coal forms after millions of years by the decay and burial of plants that grow in freshwater swamps. Special conditions are needed to form coal. At first, oxygen must not be present so that bacterial decay of the plants leads to the formation of peat. This is buried under more sediment and rotting plants. It undergoes chemical changes resulting first in lignite, then bituminous coal, and finally, if temperatures and pressures are high enough, anthracite coal.

Modern mining
Most coal is extracted by deep mining.

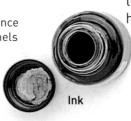
Hard labour
Coal wagons were once hauled through tunnels by people. Today, conveyor belts or trucks pulled by engines are used.

Impression of lycopod bark

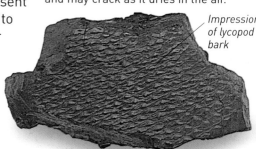

Bituminous coal
Black bituminous coal is the most common coal for household fires. This impression of a Carboniferous lycopod tree shows the plant origin of the coal.

Ink

Shoe polish

Coal content
Most coal is burnt to give heat in household fires, or to make steam, which drives power station generators to produce electricity. Many everyday products are also made from coal, such as coal-tar soap, ink, and shoe polish.

Coal-tar soap

Anthracite
Anthracite is a hard, intensely black and shiny coal. It is the best-quality coal.

Oil plant

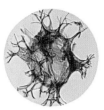

This fossil of a microscopic Eocene plant that lived in the sea has been greatly enlarged. Fossilized remains provide clues about rocks, which help geologists searching for oil.

From plankton to oil

Oil and natural gas are together known as petroleum, from the Latin words *petra* (rock) and *oleum* (oil). They were formed mainly by the decomposition of tiny planktonic plants that lived near the sea surface. When they died, their remains sank to the seabed and were buried in mud. Over millions of years, this mud turned to rock and the organic remains formed specks of carbon-rich kerogen, an early stage of oil, and then oil. Oil is often found far from where it originated. It moves upwards through porous rocks that have tiny spaces into which it can seep.

No oil

This core of rock, cut during drilling for geologists to examine, does not contain any oil.

Modern oil rig

Oil-bearing

This porous core contains oil. Oil is held as tiny droplets in rock pores – similar to the way water is held in a sponge.

Three cones of the bit

Tri-cone bit

Oil drill

Drill bits cut through rock by being rotated on a hollow drill pipe, down which a fluid is pumped. This fluid lubricates and cools the bit and takes away rock fragments.

Fossils foraminifers

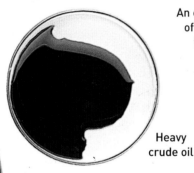

Heavy crude oil

An early way of drilling for oil

Polyester scarf

Sunglasses

Wax crayons

Micro fossils

Foraminifer fossils are microscopic animals with chalky shells.

Crude oils

It can be difficult to get oil out of rock. The presence of natural gas helps force oil to the surface, but sometimes pressure is too low and the oil must be pumped up. Crude oils (oils in their natural state) vary widely. The heaviest oils are black and thick. The lightest oils are pale and thin. All crude oils must be refined before use.

Light crude oil

Made from oil

Once in the refinery, oil is separated into liquids, gases, and solids. These make a range of products in addition to petrol, diesel, and lubricating oil. Wax crayons, sunglasses, and polyester are all by-products of oil.

Refined oil

Oils are treated in a refinery. Refining is a complex process.

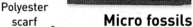

Out of the water

Colonization of the land by vertebrates, 350 million years ago, was possible through the evolution of lungs for breathing air, and limbs for walking. Air-breathing was inherited by the first land vertebrates, amphibians, from their fish ancestors. Fish with lungs for breathing – lungfish – still exist today. Limbs for walking developed from muscular fins, like those of the living coelacanth.

Fossil frog

Long hind legs

This fossil frog is a female *Discoglossus* from the Miocene Epoch of Germany. Frogs first appeared in the Triassic Period, but are seldom found fossilized because their delicate bones decay.

Curious creature

This amphibian, *Diplocaulus* (above), from the Permian of Texas, USA, lived in ponds and streams.

Eyes

Fossil tadpole

Tadpole fossils are very rare. The two eyes are visible in this Cenozoic specimen of *Pelobates*.

Water world

The axolotl is an unusual salamander from Central America. It normally remains in a "larval" stage throughout its life, using its feathery external gills to breathe underwater and not coming on land.

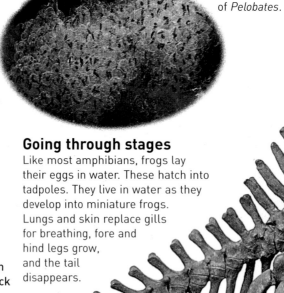

Heavy hip bones

Going through stages

Like most amphibians, frogs lay their eggs in water. These hatch into tadpoles. They live in water as they develop into miniature frogs. Lungs and skin replace gills for breathing, fore and hind legs grow, and the tail disappears.

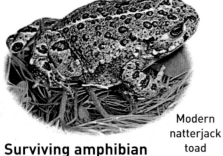

Modern natterjack toad

Surviving amphibian

Early inhabitants of the land were different from the amphibians that have survived today, such as frogs, toads, newts, and salamanders.

Strong foot

Early amphibian

An early amphibian, *Ichthyostega*, is found in Devonian rocks in Greenland. It was able to walk on land, had lungs for breathing air, but still had a tail-fin like a fish.

42

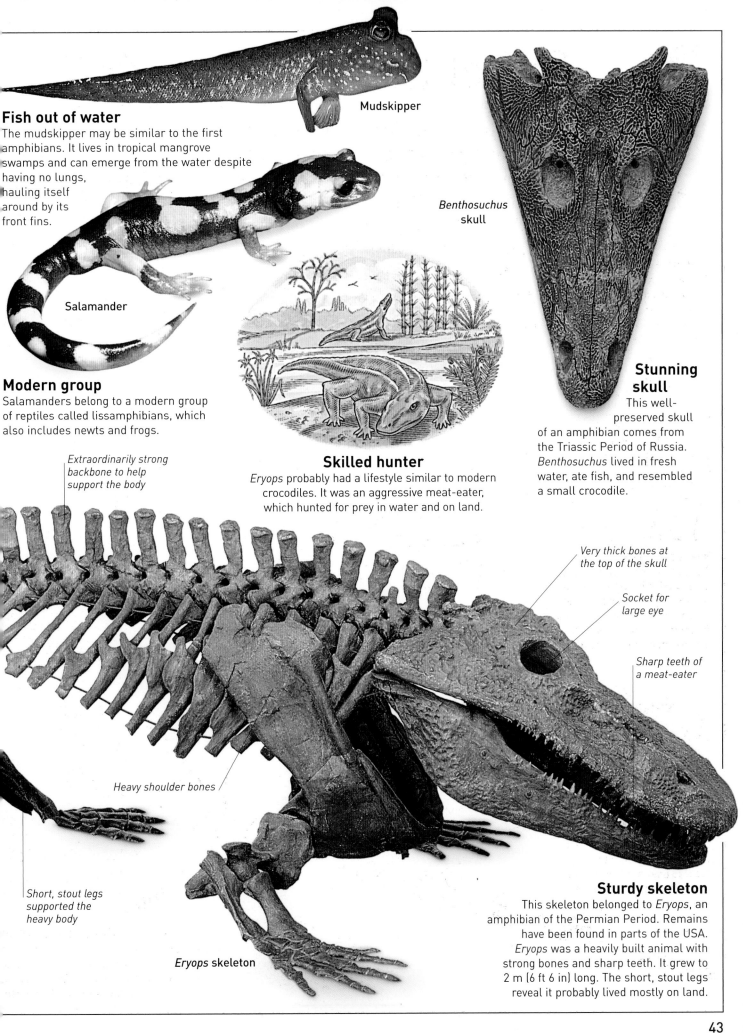

Fish out of water

The mudskipper may be similar to the first amphibians. It lives in tropical mangrove swamps and can emerge from the water despite having no lungs, hauling itself around by its front fins.

Mudskipper

Benthosuchus skull

Salamander

Modern group

Salamanders belong to a modern group of reptiles called lissamphibians, which also includes newts and frogs.

Skilled hunter

Eryops probably had a lifestyle similar to modern crocodiles. It was an aggressive meat-eater, which hunted for prey in water and on land.

Stunning skull

This well-preserved skull of an amphibian comes from the Triassic Period of Russia. *Benthosuchus* lived in fresh water, ate fish, and resembled a small crocodile.

Extraordinarily strong backbone to help support the body

Very thick bones at the top of the skull

Socket for large eye

Sharp teeth of a meat-eater

Heavy shoulder bones

Short, stout legs supported the heavy body

Eryops skeleton

Sturdy skeleton

This skeleton belonged to *Eryops*, an amphibian of the Permian Period. Remains have been found in parts of the USA. *Eryops* was a heavily built animal with strong bones and sharp teeth. It grew to 2 m (6 ft 6 in) long. The short, stout legs reveal it probably lived mostly on land.

On to the land

Three main types of reptiles live today: lizards and snakes, tortoises and turtles, and crocodiles. A fourth is represented only by the tuatara. The number of surviving reptiles is far fewer than the number of extinct forms. The first reptile fossils date from the Carboniferous Period, about 300 million years ago. Early reptiles had two features, still seen in modern species, that meant they could live away from water. They developed a special egg, known as an amniote egg, and a scaly skin to prevent their bodies drying out.

There are over 2,000 species of snakes living today.

Buried eggs

Oceanic turtles go on land to lay their eggs which they bury in sand before returning to the sea. The largest living turtle is the leatherback, which reaches 2.5 m (8 ft) in length. But the Cretaceous turtle *Archelon* grew to more than 4 m (13 ft) long

Body guard

Trionyx is a turtle from the Eocene. Only the protective carapace, or shell, is preserved here. The first turtles appeared in the Triassic Period and lacked the ability of modern species to withdraw their head, limbs, and tail completely.

Modern ladder snake

Ready for land

Turtle eggs contain liquid and have leathery shells for protection. Before birth, an embryo can develop into an animal that can breathe and live on land.

Legless vertebrate

The earliest fossil snakes come from the late Cretaceous. Snakes have a poor fossil record, but vertebrae are occasionally found. These vertebrae of *Palaeophis*, from the Palaeocene Epoch of Mali, were found separately, but have been assembled to give an idea of a snake's backbone. Snakes probably evolved from a lizard-like ancestor with their limbs getting smaller and smaller and eventually disappearing altogether.

Sprawler

Semi-improved

Fully improved

Perfect posture

The limb positions of reptiles gradually improved to support body weight more efficiently. Lizards are "sprawlers", while crocodiles have a "semi-improved" posture and can lift their bellies to move quickly. "Fully improved" animals include dinosaurs and advanced mammals.

Flattened skull

Long body

Scaly skin prevents drying out

Powerful jaws

Baby predator

Crocodiles have changed little since the Jurassic – they all have long bodies, short legs, a flattened skull, and sharp teeth. Crocodiles are predators that swim slowly towards their prey before making a rapid grab using their powerful jaws.

Diplocynodon skull

Crocodile head

The largest fossil crocodile, *Deinosuchus*, from the Cretaceous Period of Texas, USA, is estimated to have been 12–15 m (40–50 ft) long! This head belonged to an Oligocene crocodile, *Diplocynodon*.

Diagrams of a modern lizard

Long lizard

Lizards live in dry, upland areas where burial is unlikely so fossil examples are rare. The earliest finds are from the Triassic Period, and they were probably present in vast numbers with their larger relatives, the dinosaurs. This fossil lizard, *Adriosaurus*, had a long body and is almost snake-like.

Sea-dragons

During Mesozoic times, when dinosaurs roamed the land, the seas were inhabited by giant reptiles known as sea-dragons. The most numerous were the ichthyosaurs and plesiosaurs, but a third group, the mosasaurs, became common at the end of the Mesozoic Era. They lived like modern marine mammals, such as small whales, dolphins, and seals. Some ate fish, while others ate belemnites and other molluscs. They all breathed air and so surfaced regularly.

Mary Anning
Mary Anning (1799–1847) is famous for collecting fossils in Lyme Regis, on the south coast of England. These cliffs contain abundant fossils of animals that lived in the sea in Jurassic times. Mary and her brother excavated an ichthyosaur.

A good likeness
The shape of modern dolphins and ichthyosaurs suggests they shared a similar lifestyle.

Dorsal fin for steering

Backbone

Kink in backbone

Powerful tail for swimming

Pointed tooth

A mosasaur

Excavation of a mosasaur jaw from a chalk mine at Maastricht in the Netherlands, in the 18th century

Giant lizard jaw
Three teeth are visible in this mosasaur jaw fragme from the Cretaceous Period. Mosasaurs were relate to today's monitor lizards. Mosasaurs grew to 9 m (30 ft) and were slow-moving predators.

Ring of bones around eye socket to improve focus

Short, sharp teeth

Samuel Clarke

Samuel Clarke (1815–1898) was a geologist who lived near Lyme Regis. He helped professionals find sea-dragons, and is seen here holding a plesiosaur skull in 1863.

Packed teeth

The long jaws of most ichthyosaurs were full of sharp teeth. Nostrils were positioned far back on the top of the skull, as in modern dolphins and whales, making it easier to breathe when they surfaced for air.

Battle of the sea-dragons

This picture shows a fictitious fight between an ichthyosaur and a plesiosaur.

Neck vertebrae close together

Long jaws

Eye socket   *Packed teeth*

Streamlined predator

The streamlined shape of an ichthyosaur is seen in this Jurassic specimen where soft tissue has been preserved with the skeleton. The neck vertebrae of ichthyosaurs were close together so the head ran smoothly into the body. This is typical of fast-swimming predators and is seen in dolphins today. Ichthyosaurs swam by moving their tails. Their backbones had a kink as they continued to the lower part of the tail fin. The dorsal fin and paddles were used for steering and stability.

Paddle for steering

Paddle power

The limbs of plesiosaurs formed large paddles. Like a turtle, a plesiosaur probably flapped these up and down for swimming.

Main age

Dating from the Triassic Period, ichthyosaurs were most common in the Jurassic Period.

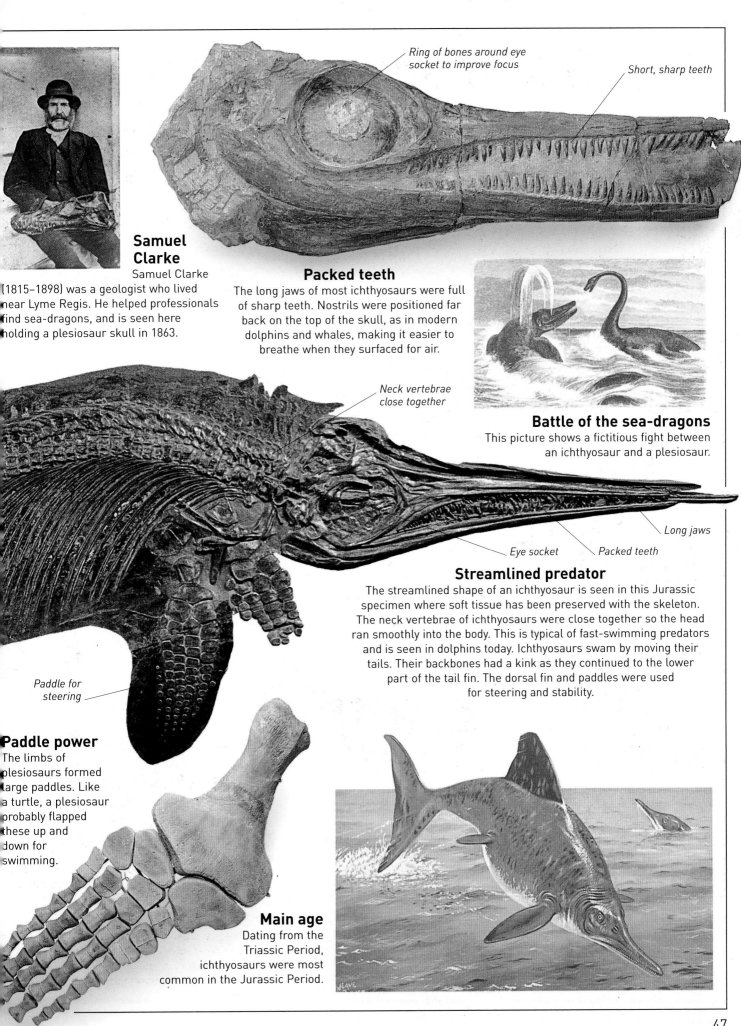

Fossil giants

Dinosaurs are probably the most impressive fossils. There were many species, and their reign spanned 150 million years from the Triassic to the Cretaceous periods. Dinosaurs were reptiles. Some ate meat, while others ate plants. Some had armoured plates, but others had spiked or clubbed tails. The extinction of the dinosaurs at the end of Cretaceous times has produced many theories, such as a change in climate or a meteor impact.

Food grinder
Jurassic sauropod *Apatosaurus* weighed 30 tonnes. Like all sauropods, it was a plant eater, using its long neck to reach treetops. It swallowed stones to help grind up food in the stomach like crocodiles do today.

Monster-stalking
Some people still search for living examples of dinosaurs.

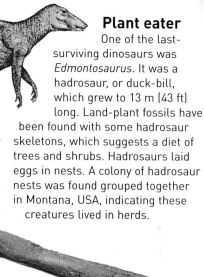

Plant eater
One of the last-surviving dinosaurs was *Edmontosaurus*. It was a hadrosaur, or duck-bill, which grew to 13 m (43 ft) long. Land-plant fossils have been found with some hadrosaur skeletons, which suggests a diet of trees and shrubs. Hadrosaurs laid eggs in nests. A colony of hadrosaur nests was found grouped together in Montana, USA, indicating these creatures lived in herds.

Edmontosaurus

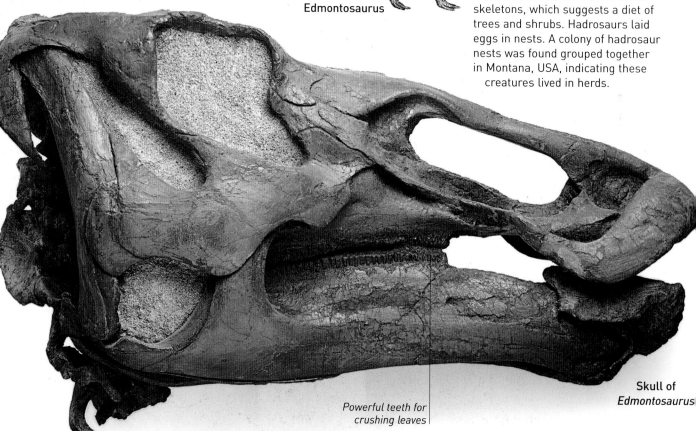

Powerful teeth for crushing leaves

Skull of *Edmontosaurus*

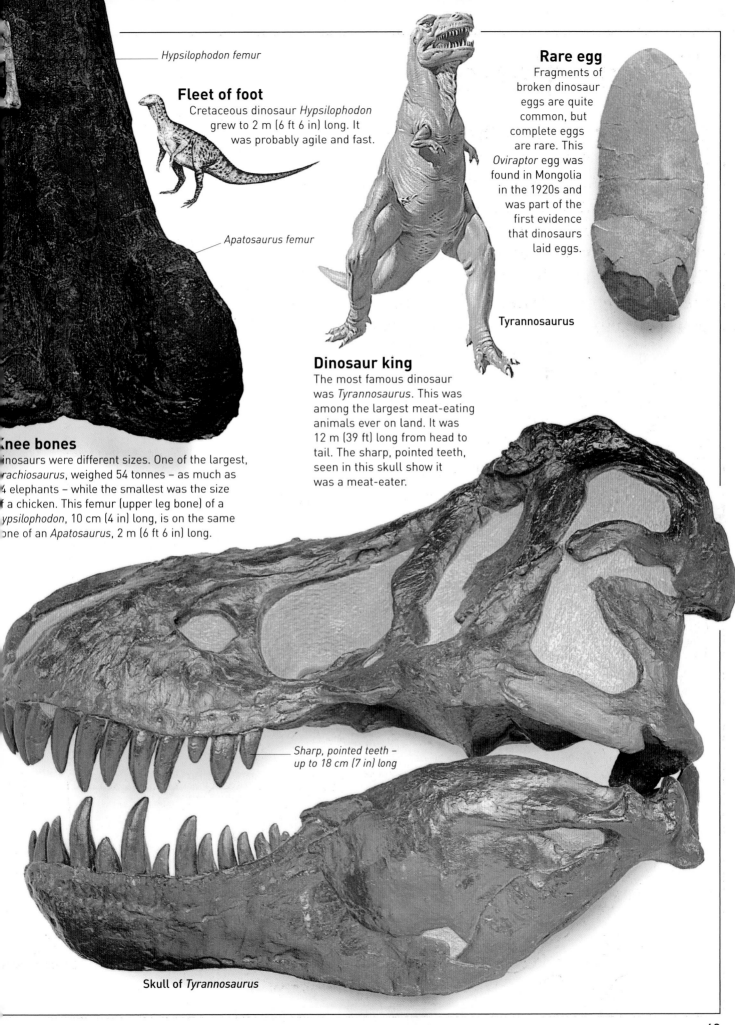

Hypsilophodon femur

Fleet of foot
Cretaceous dinosaur *Hypsilophodon* grew to 2 m (6 ft 6 in) long. It was probably agile and fast.

Apatosaurus femur

Rare egg
Fragments of broken dinosaur eggs are quite common, but complete eggs are rare. This *Oviraptor* egg was found in Mongolia in the 1920s and was part of the first evidence that dinosaurs laid eggs.

Tyrannosaurus

Dinosaur king
The most famous dinosaur was *Tyrannosaurus*. This was among the largest meat-eating animals ever on land. It was 12 m (39 ft) long from head to tail. The sharp, pointed teeth, seen in this skull show it was a meat-eater.

Knee bones
Dinosaurs were different sizes. One of the largest, *Brachiosaurus*, weighed 54 tonnes – as much as 14 elephants – while the smallest was the size of a chicken. This femur (upper leg bone) of a *Hypsilophodon*, 10 cm (4 in) long, is on the same one of an *Apatosaurus*, 2 m (6 ft 6 in) long.

Sharp, pointed teeth – up to 18 cm (7 in) long

Skull of *Tyrannosaurus*

Dinosaur discovery

The first descriptions of dinosaur fossil bones were made over 150 years ago. Teeth and bones of *Iguanodon* were found in England by Doctor Gideon Mantell. Bones of *Megalosaurus* and *Hylaeosaurus* were later discovered. In 1841 British anatomist Sir Richard Owen devised the name dinosaur, meaning "terrible lizard". Huge numbers of dinosaur remains were found in North America in the 19th century, while other finds were made in Tanzania, China, Mongolia, and Argentina. Dinosaur discoveries continue to be found.

Claw find
Bill Walker with the claw bone of *Baryonyx*, which he discovered in 1983.

Mantell's tooth!
This is one of the original *Iguanodon* teeth named by Gideon Mantell in 1825.

Mantell's quarry
Mantell was a doctor and fossil collector. The *Iguanodon* teeth and bones he described came from a quarry in Cuckfield, England, where rocks of early Cretaceous age were dug for use as gravel.

Big reptile
In 1824, William Buckland discovered dinosaur bones in Stonesfield in Oxfordshire, England. He called the animal *Megalosaurus*, which means "big reptile". This jaw bone belonged to a *Megalosaurus* and comes from the same area as Buckland's specimens.

Big and bigger
Megalosaurus was a Jurassic meat-eater related to the larger and better known *Tyrannosaurus*.

Edward Drinker Cope
From 1870 Cope took part in the great dinosaur gold rush of Montana and Wyoming in the USA. Two men are associated with this gold rush – Cope and Marsh. Both hired collectors to excavate dinosaur bones in a race to describe new species.

Fierce rivals
In this cartoon, Othniel Charles Marsh is depicted as a circus ringmaster leading his team of prehistoric animals. The rivalry between Cope and Marsh caused the two men to insult each other.

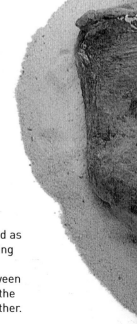

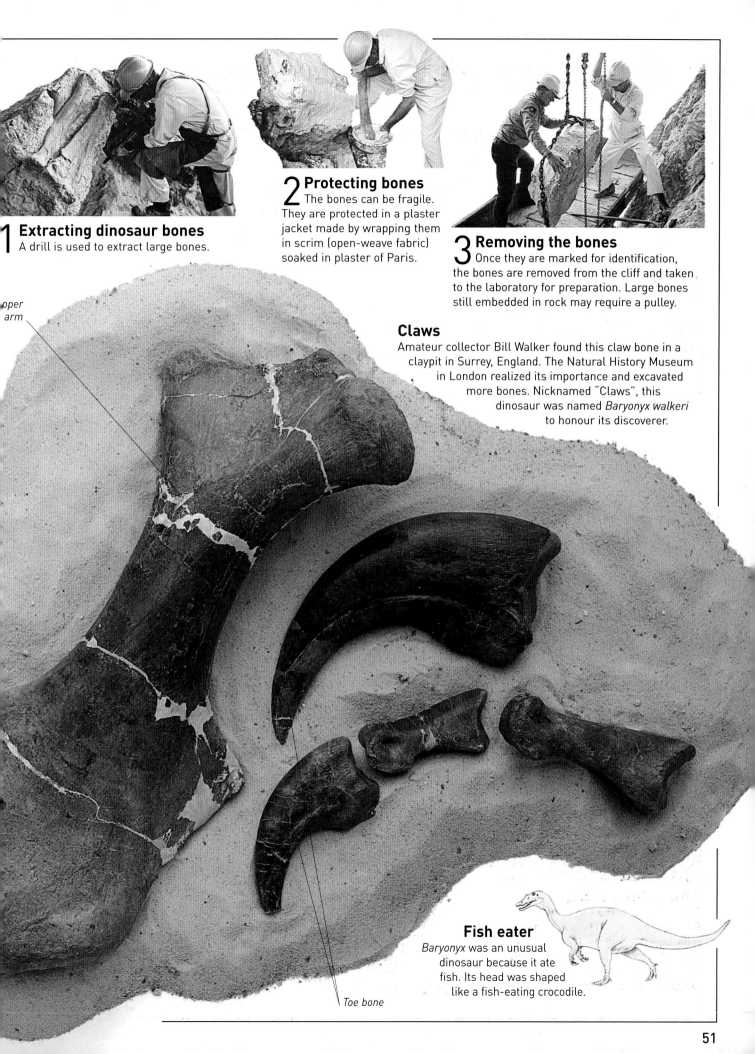

1 Extracting dinosaur bones
A drill is used to extract large bones.

2 Protecting bones
The bones can be fragile. They are protected in a plaster jacket made by wrapping them in scrim (open-weave fabric) soaked in plaster of Paris.

3 Removing the bones
Once they are marked for identification, the bones are removed from the cliff and taken to the laboratory for preparation. Large bones still embedded in rock may require a pulley.

Claws
Amateur collector Bill Walker found this claw bone in a claypit in Surrey, England. The Natural History Museum in London realized its importance and excavated more bones. Nicknamed "Claws", this dinosaur was named *Baryonyx walkeri* to honour its discoverer.

Upper arm

Fish eater
Baryonyx was an unusual dinosaur because it ate fish. Its head was shaped like a fish-eating crocodile.

Toe bone

Winged wonders

Insects were the first animals to fly more than 300 million years ago. Flying vertebrates appeared almost 100 million years later. Flapping flight evolved in three groups of vertebrates: extinct pterosaurs, birds, and bats. Pterosaurs were reptiles related to dinosaurs, with a long fourth finger to support the wing. Bird wings are supported by the fingers and forearm. Bats have wings supported by four fingers. Bones of flying vertebrates are light and fragile, so they are rarely fossilized.

Wing support
This long fingerbone supported the wing of a *Pteranodon*, one of the largest flying animals.

Well-balanced
Pteranodon was a pterosaur with a bony crest on its head that counterbalanced its long toothless beak. It was a fish-eater that flew over the sea like the modern albatross.

Story time
Pterosaur remains fuelled the imagination of authors of science fiction stories.

Furry reptile
The small Jurassic pterosaur *Pterodactylus* had membranous wings, claws, and a furry body. Evidence for fur comes from pterosaurs found in Kazakhstan with hair-like impressions around the body. This suggests that pterosaurs were warm-blooded and used fur as insulation. Pterosaurs appeared in the Triassic Period and were extinct by the end of the Cretaceous Period.

Toothed beak

Greatly lengthened fourth finger

Membranous wing

Body covered by fine fur

Short tail

Mistaken identity
This dinosaur is one that scientists believe was an ancestor of birds. In 1973 German experts found a specimen identified a *Compsognathus* wa an *Archaeopteryx*

Flying mammal
Bats are similar to pterosaurs. Bats date from the Eocene Epoch. As they roost in caves, their fossil bones can often be found in cave deposits.

Claws

Impression of feathers like a bird's

Clawed fingers like a reptile's

Teeth unlike a modern bird

Archaeopteryx had a wingspan of 50 cm (20 in)

Fossil feather

Modern bird's feather

The first bird

Archaeopteryx lived 150 million years ago. Specimens are considered the world's most precious fossils. Only five more have been found since this first one in 1861, now on display in the Natural History Museum in Berlin.

Rare find

Feathers are seldom fossilized. Occasionally they are found in fine-grained sediments such as this Oligocene limestone.

Bony tail like a reptile's

Claws

Ostrich

Enormous egg

The Madagascan elephant bird *Aepyornis maximus* was 2 m (6 ft 6 in) tall. Its fossil eggs are the largest birds' eggs known. It is compared here with an ostrich egg, one of the largest modern birds' eggs.

Ostrich egg

Fine skull

Fossilized bird remains are rare. This Eocene skull comes from the bird *Prophaethon*.

Modern tropic bird

Elephant bird egg

Elephant bird

Mammal variety

Animals as varied as mice, elephants, kangaroos, bats, cats, whales, and humans are all mammals. They are warm-blooded and produce milk to suckle their infants. Most give birth to live young, have hairy skins, complex teeth, and are highly active. The first mammals appeared at the same time as the earliest dinosaurs, 200 million years ago. Nearly all Mesozoic mammals were small shrew-like animals, but in the Cenozoic Era they diversified into the many types we know today. Complete fossil mammals are rare; many species are known only from their teeth.

Chisel-like incisor teeth

Skull of *Ischyromys*

Modern squirrel

Berries

Rodents
Rodents include rats, mice, and squirrels. Their large, chisel-like incisor teeth grow continuously. Rodents date from Palaeocene times. This is *Ischyromys* from the famous Oligocene mammal beds of the White River Badlands in the USA.

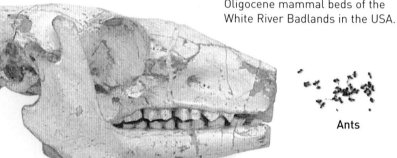

Ants

Skull of *Orycteropus*

Insect-eaters
Insect-eating mammals are generally small and include shrews and moles. *Orycteropus* was a Miocene aardvark, a kind of anteater. Mammals that eat ants have a long hard palate in the roof of the mouth to prevent ants entering the windpipe.

Modern aardvark

Modern camel

Ice-age mammal
Mammoths were elephant-like mammals adapted to life in cold climates during the Pleistocene Ice Ages. Some skeletons have been found preserved in Siberia.

Skull of *Cainotherium*

High-crowned cheek teeth

Plant-eaters
Many herbivorous mammals have cheek teeth capable of withstanding wear caused by constant chewing. Browsers eat mostly leaves, while grazers eat mostly grass. *Cainotherium* was a rabbit-like browser whose closest, but distant, living relative is a camel.

Ridges of hard enamel

Grinding tooth
Massive mammoths needed to eat large quantities of vegetation. Their huge high-crowned cheek teeth, like this one, had ridges of hard enamel to grind up vegetation.

Leaves

Skull of
Proconsul

Fruit-eaters

Monkeys, apes, and humans belong to a group of mammals called primates. Many primates are omnivores and so have a mixed diet, but some eat mostly fruit. This skull of the Miocene ape *Proconsul* has blunt teeth typical of fruit-eaters. As fruit is poor in protein, *Proconsul* may have supplemented its diet with leaves from the trees.

Modern monkey

*Blunt teeth typical
of a fruit eater*

Fruit

Nuts

Eocene landscape

Mammals became common in the Eocene Epoch. Many of the mammals that roamed the land belonged to groups with no living descendants.

Skull of
Hoplophoneus

Large canine tooth

Meat

Sabretooth cat

Meat-eaters

Carnivorous mammals have large canine teeth. These were developed to their greatest extent in the upper jaws of the sabretooths. They may have used their long teeth to stab their prey. This skull is *Hoplophoneus* from the Oligocene Epoch.

*Canine
tooth*

Skull of *Potamotherium*

Fish-eaters

Potamotherium lived in freshwater lakes in the early Miocene Epoch and fed on fish. It was similar to a modern otter, but was better adapted to life in water. It may have been a forerunner of seals, which first became common in the sea during the late Miocene.

Fish

Modern otters

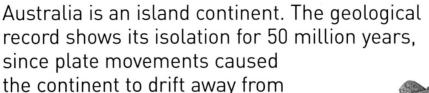

A world apart

Australia is an island continent. The geological record shows its isolation for 50 million years, since plate movements caused the continent to drift away from Antarctica. This is why many native mammals in Australia are unique. Marsupials differ from other mammals in that they have pouches where the young are reared after birth. The fleshy pouches do not fossilize, but features of the bones and teeth distinguish marsupial fossils from those of placentals. There are still many species of pouched mammal in Australia, including the kangaroo and koala.

A boxing kangaroo

Hip bone connecting the leg to the spine

Two front teeth

This skeleton of the extinct marsupial *Diprotodon* is about 3 m (10 ft) long. Its name, meaning "two front teeth", refers to the large, rodent-like incisors used for cropping vegetation. The pair of epipubic bones in the pelvic area can be used to distinguish pouched from placental mammals. *Diprotodon* comes from Pleistocene rocks and may have been hunted by early Australians – some animals in Aboriginal paintings could be *Diprotodon*.

60 million years ago

Australia

Antarctica

45 million years ago

Australia

Antarctica

Tail vertebrae

Epipubic bones helped support the pouch

Drifting continents

These two maps show the position of Australia about 60 million years ago and 45 million years ago after the split from Antarctica. The isolation of Australia prevented its colonization by placental mammals, apart from some bats and rodents. These might otherwise have replaced the native animals. This is probably what happened to the marsupials of South America, such as the extinct sabretooth *Thylacosmilus*, when placental mammals invaded South America after North and South America were joined.

Giant wombat?

Diprotodon was a herbivore It probably looked like a long-legged wombat

56

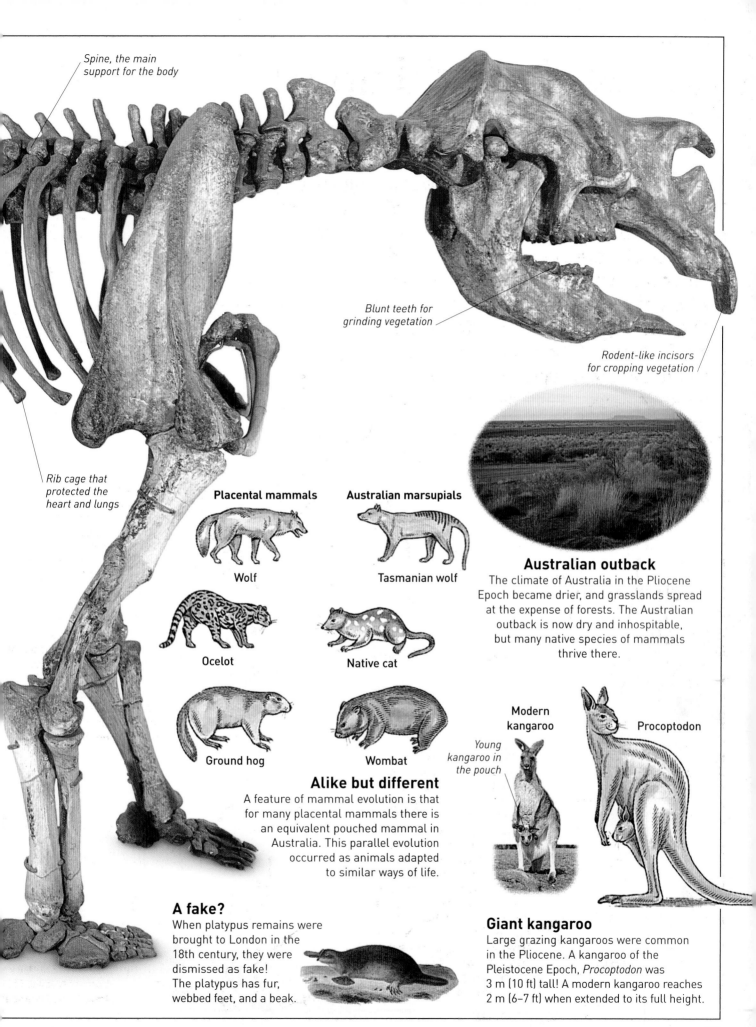

Spine, the main support for the body

Blunt teeth for grinding vegetation

Rodent-like incisors for cropping vegetation

Rib cage that protected the heart and lungs

Placental mammals

Wolf

Ocelot

Ground hog

Australian marsupials

Tasmanian wolf

Native cat

Wombat

Australian outback
The climate of Australia in the Pliocene Epoch became drier, and grasslands spread at the expense of forests. The Australian outback is now dry and inhospitable, but many native species of mammals thrive there.

Alike but different
A feature of mammal evolution is that for many placental mammals there is an equivalent pouched mammal in Australia. This parallel evolution occurred as animals adapted to similar ways of life.

Modern kangaroo

Procoptodon

Young kangaroo in the pouch

A fake?
When platypus remains were brought to London in the 18th century, they were dismissed as fake! The platypus has fur, webbed feet, and a beak.

Giant kangaroo
Large grazing kangaroos were common in the Pliocene. A kangaroo of the Pleistocene Epoch, *Procoptodon* was 3 m (10 ft) tall! A modern kangaroo reaches 2 m (6–7 ft) when extended to its full height.

Human fossils

Fossils of people (hominids) are rare and fragmentary. They teach us about the origin and development of modern people. The story begins with the ape-like *Ardipithecus* and *Australopithecus*, and ends with *Homo sapiens*. The nearest living relatives of humans are the African Great Apes (chimpanzees and gorillas), but humans have a larger brain and walk on two legs rather than four. Fossil hominids reveal how differences evolved over time.

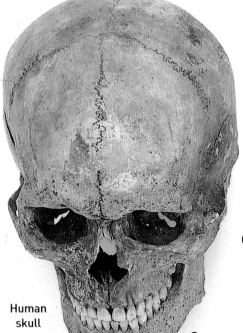

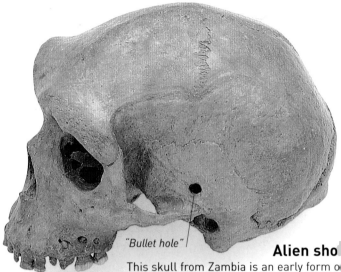

"Bullet hole"

Alien sho

This skull from Zambia is an early form o *Homo sapien*. One writer claimed the hol was a bullet shot by an alien 120,00 years ago! In fact it is an abscess

Adult's footprint

Child's footprint

First steps

These fossil footprints in Tanzania came from two-footed hominids. They were probably two adults and a child *Australopithecus* walking over damp volcanic ash. The ash hardened and was buried under more ash and sediment. They prove that a species of primate walked on two feet at least 3.6 million years ago.

Chimpanzee skull

Human skull

Comparing features

These skulls of a human and a chimpanzee look similar, but there are differences. Humans have larger brains. The average volume of a human's brain is 1,400 cubic centimetres (cc), but a chimp's brain is 400 cc. The domed human cranium can house a bigger brain. The teeth are different. A chimp cannot move its jaws side to side when chewing as its canine teeth overlap.

Carved reindeer

Antler ar

This sculpted antler is 12,000 years old and shows a male reindeer following a female. I was carved using simple flint tools This shows the development of ar and culture that is unique to humans

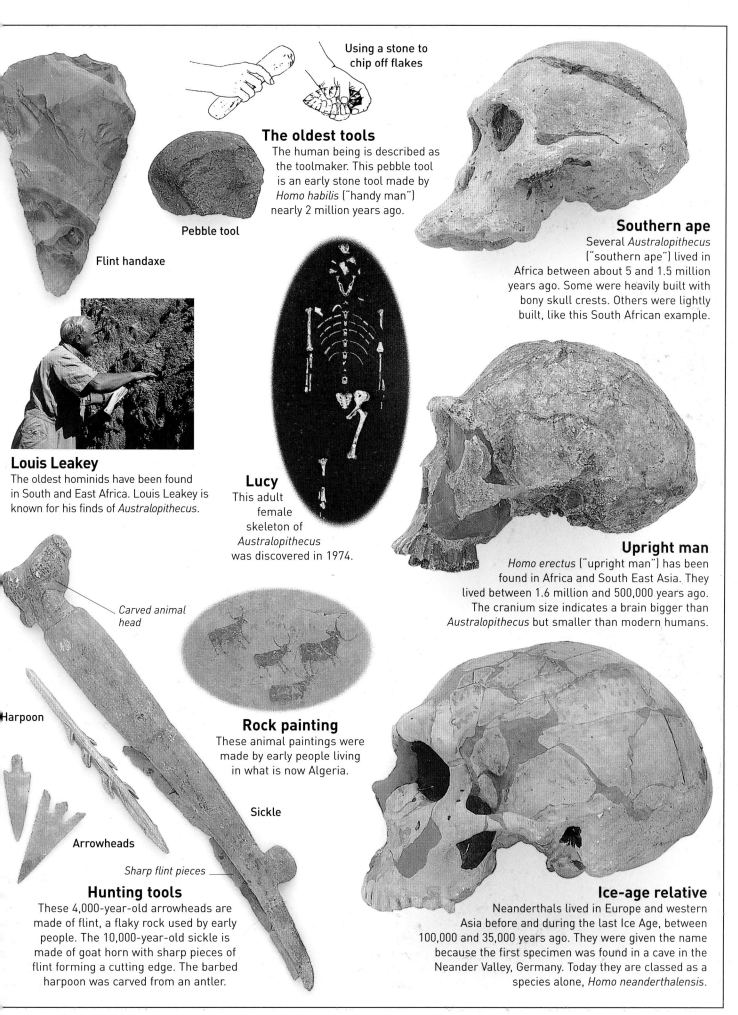

Using a stone to chip off flakes

The oldest tools

The human being is described as the toolmaker. This pebble tool is an early stone tool made by *Homo habilis* ("handy man") nearly 2 million years ago.

Pebble tool

Flint handaxe

Southern ape

Several *Australopithecus* ("southern ape") lived in Africa between about 5 and 1.5 million years ago. Some were heavily built with bony skull crests. Others were lightly built, like this South African example.

Louis Leakey

The oldest hominids have been found in South and East Africa. Louis Leakey is known for his finds of *Australopithecus*.

Lucy

This adult female skeleton of *Australopithecus* was discovered in 1974.

Upright man

Homo erectus ("upright man") has been found in Africa and South East Asia. They lived between 1.6 million and 500,000 years ago. The cranium size indicates a brain bigger than *Australopithecus* but smaller than modern humans.

Carved animal head

Harpoon

Rock painting

These animal paintings were made by early people living in what is now Algeria.

Sickle

Arrowheads

Sharp flint pieces

Hunting tools

These 4,000-year-old arrowheads are made of flint, a flaky rock used by early people. The 10,000-year-old sickle is made of goat horn with sharp pieces of flint forming a cutting edge. The barbed harpoon was carved from an antler.

Ice-age relative

Neanderthals lived in Europe and western Asia before and during the last Ice Age, between 100,000 and 35,000 years ago. They were given the name because the first specimen was found in a cave in the Neander Valley, Germany. Today they are classed as a species alone, *Homo neanderthalensis*.

Living fossils

Fossils show us that since life on Earth began, animals and plants have changed enormously. Some have changed so much that modern species are different from their fossil ancestors. There are also animals and plants living today that are almost identical with ancient fossils. The most striking examples of these "living fossils" are those animals and plants that are rare nowadays, especially those like the coelacanth and slit shells, which were known as fossils before they were discovered to be still living.

Sole survivor
The tuatara is the only survivor of a group of reptiles in Triassic times. It inhabits a few islands off New Zealand.

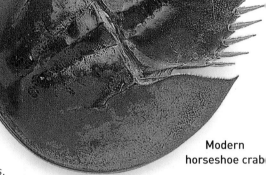

Fossil horseshoe crab

False crabs
These are not true crabs, but are related to spiders and scorpions. The modern horseshoe crab, *Limulus*, lives near shorelines in the Far East and the Atlantic Ocean off North America. It is similar to the fossil *Mesolimulus*, a marine animal from 150 million years ago.

Modern horseshoe crab

Modern cockroaches

Ancient insect
Still common today, cockroaches, together with dragonflies, are among the oldest insects and date back to the Carboniferous Period.

Fossil cockroach

Fan-shaped leaves

Ginkgo leaf

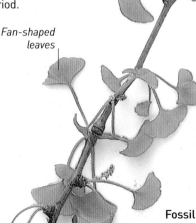

Fossil *Ginkgo*

Modern *Ginkgo* branch

Lone ranger
Ginkgos appeared in the Triassic and were more widespread in the past than they are today. Only a single species, *Ginkgo biloba*, lives today. Known as the maidenhair tree, it grows in western China. The fan-shaped leaves are easily recognizable when fossilized, as in this Jurassic example.

Ancient mammal

Didelphids, including the opossums, are pouched mammals from the Americas. Among mammals, didelphids are very old. They are first recorded in the Cretaceous Period of North America. Modern opossums have many features typical of the related primitive didelphids of the Cretaceous age.

Fossil slit shell

Modern Virginia opossum

Variety of teeth indicating a mixed diet

Fossil skull of a didelphid

Modern slit shell

Back to life

Snails belonging to *Pleurotomaria*, the slit shells, are rare today. Living examples were first discovered in 1856 at depths beyond 200 m (650 ft). Almost identical shells had long been known as fossils.

Slit in shell

Three-lobed tail

Fossil coelacanth

Wedgwood plate commemorating the catching of a live coelacanth

Commemorative stamps from the Comoro Islands

Presumed dead

The most famous of all living fossils is the coelacanth. Coelacanths have a three-lobed tail and fins with arm-like bases. They range back to the Devonian Period. It was thought that coelacanths had become extinct in Cretaceous times until a living one was caught off the South African coast in 1938. Some have been photographed alive in water off the Comoro Islands, north-east of Madagascar. In 1998 a new species of coelacanth was found off the Indonesian coast.

Modern coelacanth

Wanted!

The first modern coelacanth was identified in 1938 by Professor Smith in South Africa. He offered £100 for a second one, which he received in 1952.

61

Fossil hunting

Fossil collecting is a hobby that requires only basic tools. Sea cliffs, quarries, and other rock exposures provide productive places for fossil collectors. It may be necessary to get permission to collect from land owners, and over-collecting in one area is best avoided.

An historic find?

Chisels
A hammer and chisel can help to extract fossils from their matrix (surrounding rock).

Hammer for use with a chisel

Field notebook
Rock formations and locality of finds should be recorded in a field notebook.

Hammers
A geological hammer can be used to break up rocks.

Standard geological hammer

Trowels
Fossils in soft sediment can be removed using a trowel.

Fossil map
Geological maps help to locate promising places to collect fossils, as they identify the names and ages of rocks.

Hand lens
A pocket hand lens with a magnification of 10 to 20 times is valuable for examining fossils in the field.

Brushes
These brushes can remove sediment during excavation of fossils from soft rocks.

Safety helmet

Sieve for separating out small fossils

Bivalve

Brachiopod

HINOID
Iicraster
etaceous

Cha Engiana

Drawer of specimens
After cleaning with water, fossils should be stored with care. Cardboard trays are good for holding labelled fossils.

Echinoid

ONITE
oboceras nathorsti
ssic. Kimm

CORAL
eliasorae
liocene
e Pelou
France

Coral

Echinoid

Ammonite

In the field
This boy should be wearing a helmet to hammer fossils out of the rock. Care should be taken when fossil collecting. A safety helmet is a must.

Close study
A magnifying glass or a binocular microscope is best for close study.

BRACHIOPOD
Sphaeroidothyris sphaeroidalis

Jurassic. Bajocian
Upper Inferior Oolite
East Cliff, Burbon
Bradstock, Dorset,
England

Labels
Labelling fossil specimens is essential, including the rock formation and location. Fossils can be numbered with sticky labels.

Brushes and dental picks for fossil preparation

Microscope slides
Small fossils can be kept in wooden or cardboard cavity slides, so they can be looked at under a microscope. They should be stuck down or secured beneath a transparent cover glass.

Canvas bag for larger fossils

Drawings
Drawings enhance fossil collections. These books were compiled over a century ago.

Plastic pots for collecting small fossils

Goggles

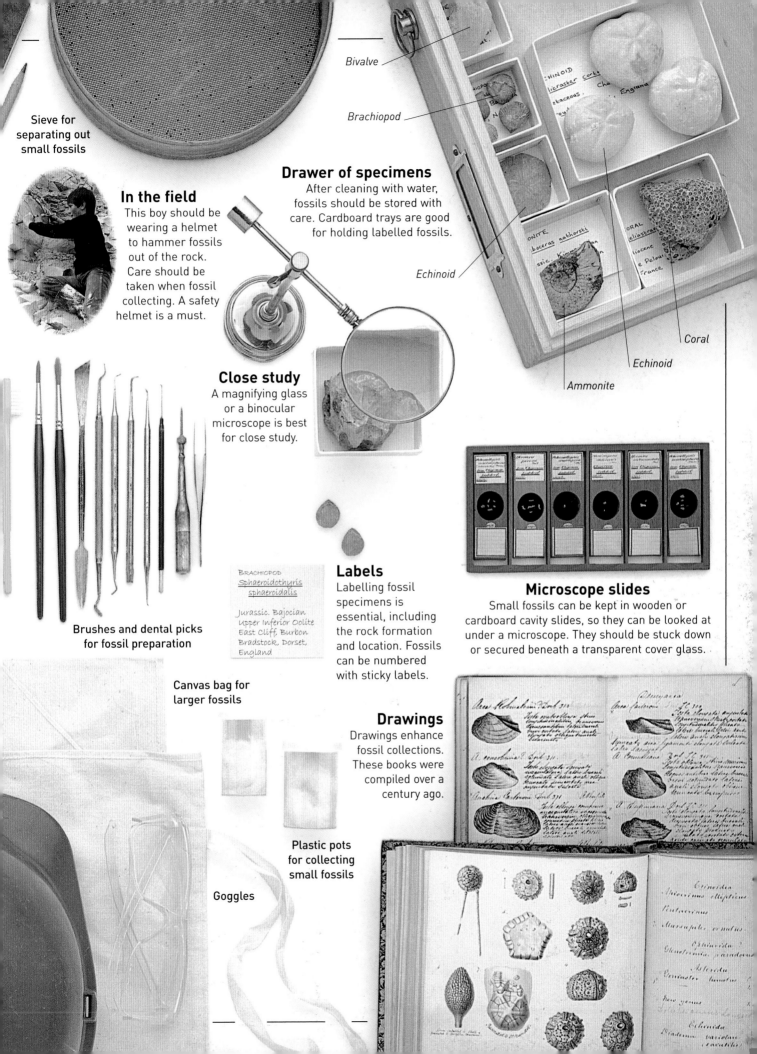

Did you know?

Amazing Facts

Dromaeosaur fossil

In the 1990s, palaeontologists began to dig up fossils of feathered dinosaurs in China – the best evidence yet that dinosaurs may have evolved into birds. Dromaeosaurs were small, fast-moving meat-eaters that had primitive feathers.

The first fossils of the arthropod *Anomalocaris* were limbs, jaws, or other body parts. The huge front limbs were thought to be tails from an extinct shrimp. It was only when a complete fossil was found that scientists put together this creature.

Anomodonts are the most primitive beasts with mammal characteristics that we know. The 260-million-year-old skull of one was found in South Africa in 1999. About the size of sheep, anomodonts were plant-eaters that lived long before the dinosaurs. They had some reptilian characteristics, and some mammalian.

Fossils of an early whale, *Ambulocetus*, show that it was about 3 m (10 ft) long and looked like a big, furry crocodile! Although it had the teeth and skull of a whale and was an excellent swimmer, it also had legs for walking on land. Its name means "walking whale".

Opalized brachiopod

At Holzmaden, Germany, there are fossils of thousands of Jurassic marine creatures. One amazing fossil is an ichthyosaur in the act of giving birth.

Australia has large opal deposits that formed in the early Cretaceous Period. During mining

Fossilized insect and spider in amber

for opal gems, specimens of opalized shellfish have been found. One of the finest opal fossils is "Eric", a complete pliosaur skeleton (below). Pliosaurs were marine reptiles that lived at the time of the dinosaurs.

In the *Jurassic Park* films, DNA from the bodies of insects fossilized in amber was used to reconstruct whole herds of dinosaurs. Scientists have extracted DNA in this way, but only fragments of it – not enough to rebuild prehistoric animals.

The first complete Pleistocene animal was excavated in 1999 by French palaeontologist Bernard Buigues. The Siberian woolly mammoth had lain frozen for over 20,000 years. It was named "Jarkov", after the family who discovered it.

"Eric", the opalized pliosaur

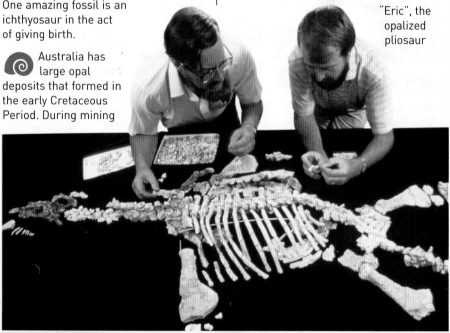

Record Breakers

EARLIEST FOSSIL EMBRYO
The earliest-known fossilized animal embryo dates back 670 million years in Guizhou province, China.

OLDEST FOSSIL FLOWER
A 125-million-year-old flowering plant, named *Archaefructus liaoningensis*, was found in Liaoning province, China, in 1998.

LARGEST-EVER LAND MAMMAL
An 83 cm (2 ft 9 in)-long skull fossil in Mongolia belonged to *Andrewsarchus*, an Eocene carnivore. It could have been 6 m (19 ft) long and weighed a tonne.

OLDEST FOSSIL FISH
Two fish, *Haikouichthys ercaicunensis* and *Myllokunmingia fengjiaoa*, were found in rocks from 530 million years ago in Yunnan, China.

Questions And Answers

Pederpes finneyae

Q Where are the oldest fossils on Earth?

A British Columbia's Burgess Shale used to be the best site for Cambrian fossils, but now older finds are coming out of sites near Kunming, in the province of Yunnan, southwest China. Preserved in rock known as the Maotianshan shales, they include the earliest examples of fish yet discovered. Thousands of near-perfect soft-bodied fossils have been found. Collectively, they are known as the "Chengjiang fauna", after a village near the sites.

Q Where in the world is the Petrified Forest?

A The Petrified Forest is a collection of fossilized logs and tree trunks in an area of national park in the Arizona desert. They date back nearly 220 million years. As well as plants, there are about 40 fossilized bee nests, the earliest ever found, and lots of bone fragments from vertebrates including dinosaurs, pterosaurs, fish, primitive reptiles, and amphibians.

Fossilized sections of tree trunk in the Petrified Forest, Arizona

Q Which animal was first to walk on land?

A The earliest fossil evidence is the skeleton of a 1-m- (3-ft-) long amphibian, *Pederpes finneyae*, that lived 345 million years ago. All the earlier feet fossils that have been found were designed to point back, and would have been used for swimming. *Pederpes'* ankle joints were evolved to take steps forwards. *Pederpes* probably

A dig in Yunnan province, China

spent some time on land, and some in the water. It lived in swamps in what is now Scotland.

Q Which American river is stocked full of fossilized fish?

A The world's richest fish fossil site is the Green River Formation at Fossil Butte National Monument, Wyoming, USA, which covers an area of 64,750 sq km (25,000 sq miles). The fossils date back some 55 million years to the Eocene Epoch, when there was a series of large inland lakes on

the site. The dead animals and plants that sank to the bottom of these lakes have been exquisitely preserved. Thousands of fish specimens have been found, as well as turtles, birds, mammals, and crocodiles.

Q Where did reptiles turn into mammals?

A Fossil hunters working in the Karoo Basin, South Africa, have found plenty of evidence of various

Diplomystus denatus, or herring, from the Green River Formation

"mammal-like" reptiles, called therapsids. These include the hippopotamus-like *Lystrosaurus*, the sabre-toothed predator *Lycaenops*, and the cat-sized *Thrinaxodon*. All of these creatures had characteristics of reptiles, but their teeth were more like those of mammals. This is exciting for scientists. By examining the therapsid fossils, they can start to understand the evolutionary changes that led to the first true mammals.

Identifying fossils

Fossils can be split into three groups: plants, animals with backbones, and animals without backbones. There are also trace fossils, such as animal tracks and coprolites.

Fake flower
This may look like a flower, but scientists think it was a primitive animal from the Precambrian seabed.

Fossil id
This page is from a book that identifies invertebrate fossil finds.

PLANT FOSSILS

Tree trunk
Whole forests of preserved tree trunks have been found fossilized, with the growth rings visible and intact.

Sequoia cone
This ironstone fossil is a pine cone from a sequoia tree. The oldest sequoia fossils date to Jurassic times.

Clubmoss
This clubmoss fossil is *Archaeosigillaria* from the Carboniferous Period. Once as tall as trees, they are now small plants.

Fern
This fern leaf was found in the Hermit Shale, USA. Fossilized soft plant parts can be found in shales and mudstones.

ANIMAL FOSSILS: VERTEBRATES

Reptile
This skeleton is of *Pachypleurosaurus*, a reptile that lived in what is now Europe, in the Middle Triassic Period.

Fish
This freshwater perch, *Priscacara*, was found in the fossil-rich Green River Formation in the USA.

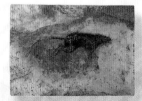

Bird
One of the world's most famous fossils, this is *Archaeopteryx*, the oldest-known bird, in limestone.

Mammal
This fossil of *Macrocranion*, an Eocene hedgehog, was found at Grube Messel, Germany.

Teeth
The vertebrate fossils that amateur hunters are most likely to find are teeth, especially shark teeth.

ANIMAL FOSSILS: INVERTEBRATES

Belemnite
Belemnites were molluscs related to modern-day squid and octopus. All that is left is the animal's inside shell.

Trilobite
Encrinurus lived in shallow seas in the Silurian Period. A head shield gave it the nickname "strawberry-headed trilobite".

Crinoid (sea lily)
Crinoids were common in the Palaeozoic seas. *Cupressocrinites* used its petal-like arms to filter food from the sea water.

Brachiopod
About 2 cm (0.75 in) long, this brachiopod is *Goniorhynchia*, which lived in the Middle Jurassic Period.

Ammonite
Gunnarites is a Late Cretaceous ammonite with a distinctive shell. This is a grey sandstone fossil.

Foraminiferan (Microfossil)
This highly-magnified image shows the fossilized test (skeleton) of tiny, single-celled protozoa *Elphidium*.

Bivalve
About 7 cm (2.75 in) long, this Jurassic oyster, called *Gryphaea*, is more popularly known as the Devil's toenail.

Coral
Colpophyllia is often called "brain coral" because of the distinctive shape formed by the colony.

Gastropod
This snail is *Pleurotomaria*, or a slit shell, with distinctive nobbly riblets. A living relative is seen on page 61.

Sponge
Early Cretaceous sponge, *Raphidonema farringdonense*, was common in shallow seas in what is now Oxfordshire, England.

Graptolite
These are *Rhabdinopora*, the earliest graptolite plankton. Graptolite fossils show a colony of creatures.

Echinoid (sea urchin)
This extinct urchin, *Phymosoma*, lived in the Cretaceous Period. Its test (skeleton) and spines have been fossilized in chalk.

Find out more

To find out more about fossils, go to local or national museums and see some spectacular collections. You could look out for television programmes about fossil hunters and their exciting new finds. Visit a library or fossil websites to read up more. You could also become a fossil hunter. It is a good idea to join a local club. Fossil-collecting is great fun, and you will soon build up your own collection.

Palaeontologists in the lab
In this French laboratory, experts are removing fossilized bones from a plaster cast. The plaster was set around the fossils at the place they were discovered to protect them during transportation. Casts are also taken of fragile fossils, for displaying.

Amateur fossil hunter
It takes a great deal of patience to be a fossil hunter. Quite often, you might come home empty-handed, so it is important to enjoy the quest for its own sake. This fossil hunter in Florida is sifting through shingle, a method suitable only for certain beaches.

Jet necklace
See how many "fossils" you can spot in a day. Amber and jet are just fossilized plant matter. Think about fossil fuels and their by-products.

Palaeontologist at work
Dinosaur National Monument, Colorado, is a protected site. Its fossilized dinosaur bones are dug out by professionals. If you want a career as a palaeontologist, aim for a science degree and gather experience on digs.

USEFUL WEBSITES

- The Earthlab datasite
  www.nhm.ac.uk/our-science/collections/
  paleontology-collections.html
- America's National Museum of Natural History
  naturalhistory.si.edu
- Links to natural history museums around the world
  www.ucmp.berkeley.edu
- Link to DK's interactive website on palaeontology and fossils
  www.dkfindout.com/uk/
  dinosaurs-and-prehistoric-life/fossils/

PLACES TO VISIT

AMERICAN MUSEUM OF NATURAL HISTORY, NEW YORK, USA
The largest collection of vertebrate fossils.
- *Buettneria*, an early four-limbed animal
- New reconstructions of *T-rex* and *Apatosaurus*

MUSEUM NATIONAL D'HISTOIRE NATURELLE, PARIS, FRANCE
A leading natural history museum.
- Gallery of specimens that chart the evolution of the vertebrate skeleton
- The world's oldest fossilized insects
- Excellent collection of plant fossils

NATIONAL MUSEUM OF NATURAL HISTORY, WASHINGTON, USA
A big collection of Burgess Shale fauna.
- Forty dinosaurs on display
- A collection of over 200,000 foraminifera

THE NATURAL HISTORY MUSEUM, LONDON, UK
This museum has dinosaur exhibits.
Attractions to look out for include:
- Huge *Diplodocus* reconstruction
- Earth Lab and its geology database

Under the microscope

At the Natural History Museum, London, visitors can handle real specimens and examine them under a microscope. There are experts on hand to help visitors identify fossils they have found. The inner gallery has a useful library of reference material.

The Cambridge Museum

Founded in 1814, the University Museum of Zoology in Cambridge, England, houses a superb collection of fossils. It includes fish from Canada and Scotland, mammals from North America, and reptiles from Africa.

Dinosaur museum

Europe's first museum dedicated to dinosaurs opened at Espéraza in France, in 1992. Many displays are fossils dug from Late Cretaceous rock deposits. The collection includes bones and eggs, like these of the titanosaur.

The Natural History Museum, Paris

The entomology gallery in France's Natural History Museum has some of the oldest fossilized insects. There is also a palaeobotany department for plant fossils.

Glossary

Anthracite

AMBER
Fossilized resin of an ancient conifer.

AMMONITE
An extinct cephalopod with a shell, common in the Mesozoic Era.

AMPHIBIAN
A cold-blooded animal adapted to life on land and in water.

ANATOMIST
Someone who studies the structure of animals.

ANGIOSPERM
A flowering plant that protects its seeds inside a fruit.

ANTHRACITE
Hard, shiny, jet-black coal.

ARTHROPOD
An animal with jointed legs, a segmented body, and an exoskeleton, such as a trilobite.

BACTERIUM
A simple living organism.

BELEMNITE
Extinct cephalopod related to the modern-day squid.

Eocene angiosperm

BIVALVE
An animal with two similar shells.

BRACHIOPOD
An animal with two shells, one slightly larger than the other.

CAMBRIAN
The geological period from 545–495 MYA.

CARBONIFEROUS
The geological period from 354–290 MYA.

CARNIVORE
An animal that eats other animals.

CENOZOIC
Our present geological era, which began 65 MYA – the age of mammals.

CEPHALOPOD
A mollusc with tentacles.

Diplomystus, or herring, from the Early Eocene

COAL MEASURE FOREST
Swampy forest where plant matter from the Carboniferous era turned into coal over time.

COPROLITE
Fossilized animal dropping.

CORAL
A build-up of polyps' skeletons.

CRETACEOUS
The last geological period of the Mesozoic, from 142–65 MYA.

CRUST
The thin outer layer of Earth.

CRUSTACEAN
An arthropod with a hard shell, jointed legs, and compound eyes.

Devonian fish

DENDRITE
A crystal that forms branches.

DEVONIAN
The geological period from 417–354 MYA.

ECHINODERM
A marine animal with five-point symmetry.

ELEMENT
Material that cannot be made into more simple substances by chemical means.

EOCENE
The geological epoch from 55–34 MYA.

EROSION
The wearing away of rock by wind, water, and ice.

EVOLUTION
The process by which species change into new ones over millions of generations.

EXOSKELETON
Tough outer casing that protects the body of some invertebrates.

FOSSIL
The naturally preserved remains of animals or plants, or evidence of them.

FOSSIL FUEL
Materials formed from the remains of ancient living things, that can be burned to give off energy, such as, oil and coal.

GEOLOGY
The study of rocks.

GYMNOSPERM
A plant that produces seeds in a cone.

HERBIVORE
Grazing or browsing animal.

HOLOCENE
Our present geological epoch, which began 10,000 years ago.

ICTHYOSAUR
An extinct reptile from the Mesozoic Era.

IGNEOUS ROCK
Rock formed as magma cooled and hardened in Earth's crust.

IMPERVIOUS
Rock that liquid cannot penetrate.

INVERTEBRATE
An animal without a backbone.

JURASSIC
The geological period from 206–142 MYA.

LIMESTONE
A sedimentary rock made of the fossilized remains of ancient creatures.

The tests (skeletons) of a fossilized sand dollar, left, and a modern sea urchin, below

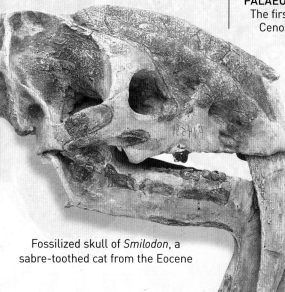

Fossilized skull of *Smilodon*, a sabre-toothed cat from the Eocene

LYCOPOD
The clubmosses, a group of primitive plants that reproduce by spores.

MAMMAL
A warm-blooded, hair-covered animal that usually gives birth to live young.

MESOZOIC
The geological era from 248–65 MYA, known as the age of the dinosaurs.

METAMORPHIC ROCK
Rock that forms due to heat and pressure, or heat alone.

MIOCENE
The geological epoch from 24–5 MYA.

MOLLUSC
An unsegmented invertebrate.

NATURALIST
Someone who studies nature.

OLIGOCENE
The geological epoch from 34–24 MYA.

ORDOVICIAN
The geological period from 495–443 MYA.

PALAEOCENE
The first geological epoch of the Cenozoic, from 65–55 MYA.

PALAEONTOLOGY
The study of fossils.

PALAEOZOIC
The geological era from 545–248 MYA.

PANGAEA
The supercontinent that formed in the Late Palaeozoic.

PERMIAN
The last geological period of the Palaeozoic, from 290–248 MYA.

PLACODERM
An extinct fish with armour and jaws.

PLEISTOCENE
The geological epoch from 2–0.01 MYA, the last Ice Age.

PLESIOSAUR
An extinct, long-necked marine reptile.

PLIOCENE
The geological epoch from 5–2 MYA.

PRECAMBRIAN
The earliest geological period, from 4,600 MYA, when Earth formed, until 545 MYA.

PTEROSAUR
An extinct flying reptile.

REPTILE
A cold-blooded, scaly animal that usually reproduces by laying eggs.

ROCK
Solid mixtures of minerals.

SEDIMENTARY ROCK
Rock that forms at Earth's surface from layers of rock fragments and other deposited substances.

SHALE
A rock made of compacted clay.

SILURIAN
The geological period from 443–417 MYA.

TEST
An echinoid's plated skeleton.

TRACE FOSSIL
Fossilized evidence of the activities of an animal, such as footprints.

TRIASSIC
The first geological period of the Mesozoic, from 248–206 MYA.

VERTEBRATE
An animal with a backbone.

A sea sponge from the Cretaceous Period

Index

Acknowledgements

Dorling Kindersley would like to thank: Plymouth Marine Laboratory, National Museum of Wales, Kew Gardens for specimens for photography; Lester Cheeseman and Thomas Keenes for additional design assistance; Anna Kunst for editorial assistance; Meryl Silbert; Karl Shone for additional photography (pp.18–19); Jane Parker for the index; and Andrea Mills for editing the relaunch version and Polly Goodman for proofreading it.

The author would like to thank: M K Howarth; C Patterson; R A Fortey; C H C Brunton; A W Gentry; B R Rosen; J B Richardson; P L Forey; N J Morris; C B Stringer; A B Smith; J E P Whittaker; R Croucher; S F Morris; C R Hill; A C Milner; R L Hodgkinson; C A Walker; R J Cleevely; C H Shute; V T Young; D N Lewis; A E

Longbottom; M Crawley; R Kruszynski; C Bell; S C Naylor; A Lum; R W Ingle; P D Jenkins; P D Hillyard; D T Moore; J W Schopf; C M Butler; P W Jackson

Picture Credits
t=top, b=bottom, m=middle, l=left, r=right

Aldus Archive: 53tm, 54bl;
Alison Anholt-White: 28tl;
Ardea: 9bl, 21m, 42m, 42bl, 43t, 61tm;
Biofotos/Heather Angel: 26m, 31mr, 39br, 44–5bm; **Booth Museum of Natural History** 66bl; **Bridgeman Art Library:** 14mr; /Musée Cluny/Lauros-Giraudon 17tl; Dept. of Earth Sciences, University of **Cambridge:** 39mr; **Cleveland Museum of Natural History, Ohio:** 59m; **Bruce Coleman:** 8br, 22m; /Jeff Foote 28tr, 39m, 40m; /Fritz Prenzel 57br; /Kim Campbell 59ml; **Simon**

Conway Morris: 20m;
Corbis: James L. Amos 65br, 68bl;
Mary Evans Picture Library: 13ml, 14br, 15tl, 20m, 48t, 52tl, 54t, 54br, 55t, 55mr, 55b, 62m; **Vivien Fifield:** 50bl;
Geological Society: 46t; **Geoscience Features Picture Library:** 9tr, 51tl, 51tm, 51tr; **David George:** 25m; **Robert Harding Picture Library:** 21br, 29m, 59b; **Michael Holford:** 12tl; **Hunterian Museum:** 66tl; **Hutchison Library:** 24tl, 57mr; **Mansell Collection:** 26t, 40b; **Natural History Museum, London:** 66tr, 70m, 66tm, 66ml, 66bm (below), 69t; / Geological Museum of China 64tl; **Oxford Scientific Films:** 44bl, 53bm; **Oxford University Museum:** 66br (above), 71tm, 71b; **Planet Earth Pictures:** 32ml, 41m, 43ml, 44mr, 63tl; **Rex Features:** Sipa Press 65m; **Ann Ronan Picture Library:** 15tm, 50br; **Royal Tyrell Museum, Canada:** 66bm (above); **Science Photo Library:** 58r; / Tony Craddock 65bl; /Peter Menzel 64br; / Philippe Plailly 68t; /Philippe Plailly/Eurelios 69ml, 69mr; /Andrew Syred 67mr (above)

Paul Taylor: 19b; **University Museum of Zoology, Cambridge:** 69b; /Sarah Finney (GLAHM 100815) 65t;
ZEFA: 20–21bl

Wallchart: Corbis: Roger Ressmeyer fcl (person); **Dorling Kindersley:** Natural History Museum, London tl/ (ammonite), ftl/ (shells and pebbles), cla, fcl/ (coral), cl/ (bryozoa), fcl, clb/ (lobster), fbl/ (tooth), tr/ (eryops), ftr/ (lizard fossil), c/ (skull), bc, cr/ (human skull), fcr/ (chimpanzee skull), crb, fbr, cr, fcr/ (t-rex), br/ (hammer), crb/ (brushes); **Getty Images:** Taxi / Peter Scoones fbr/ (blue fish)

Illustrations by: John Woodcock, Eugene Fleury

Original picture research by: Kathy Lockley

All other images © Dorling Kindersley

For further information, see:
www.dkimages.com